My Life in Baking

"I just wanted to say a very big thank you to you and Shipton Mill for the fabulous bakery course we all attended yesterday. We all found it very informative and we thoroughly enjoyed it....

"Your passion and love for the product really came through and your bakery knowledge and skills are second to none. We all talked about bread on the way home in the car and it was really good for me to hear the younger members of the brigade having such an in-depth conversation about bread and bread products."

Mark Fromont, Head Chef, Master of the Household's Department,
Buckingham Palace

Clive Mellum

My Life in Baking

Fifty years on

flankó press 2016

My life in baking: fifty years on

Clive Mellum

First published in Great Britain 2016 by flankó press

Text & photographs © Clive Mellum 2015

Cover photograph Adobe Stockphoto © Grecaud Paul

Graphics © raven, Strezhnev Pavel, Manfred Lemke

ISBN 978-0-9935405-0-9

Editor: Jonquil Hole

Design and Production: Manfred Lemke, flankopress.com

Printed and bound by Ingram Spark

My Thanks go to

My parents who instilled in me the basic values in life but gave me the freedom to grow my own personality; they also encouraged me to persevere at the early stages of my apprenticeship when the temptation to pursue the larger pay-packet by doing labouring work presented itself.

To the late Owen Shearer, an exceptionally skilled Baker I had the privilege of working with; he had a way of passing on his skills quietly but with such passion I now know you can only get from someone whose life has evolved round his trade.

To Mr Knight, my tutor at Brighton Technical College; he taught me to step aside from what is now known as dyslexia, for which I was so often ridiculed at school. This gave me the confidence to put down on paper the baking skills I had in my hands, helping me to achieve my theory exam results.

To my late Aunt Glad Byford, who had the confidence in me to stand guarantor for some of the monies needed to purchase my own bakery at the young age of 21.

To the two independent Flour Mills I worked with for over thirty years; they gave me the opportunity to extend and question my knowledge on a daily base as fluctuating flour quality issues arose, and my skills became useful to defend their reputation, helping to maintain their volume of sales and profit.

To my loyal school friend and wife of fifty years, Barbara, who never questioned my career decisions, just offered support and help with whatever I chose to do, very often finding herself spending many nights and weekends on her own with three young children as I chose to work many unpaid hours to solve baking and flour issues. She understood it was never just a job but a personal challenge for me to be able to solve problems as they arose.

To all the Bakers and Bakeries I have had the privilege of working with and in, making it possible for me to exchange ideas in life skills as well as baking skills over many years.

Through the latter years the general public for their encouragement while attending the workshops; their desire to understand my chosen industry has far outreached my expectations. This helped me to condense and translate my life's work to an understandable format easily distributed in the short time we had together around a table, or through the many many emails answered in the evenings, guiding people through their bread problems and helping them to distinguish between good and bad breads in the hopes that this trend for quality and tradition may continue by the many that choose to tread this same path.

Special thanks go Jonquil Hole who attended the workshops; her gentle personality and encouragement has made this book possible. Jonquil gave me the confidence to show her this book (which has been in the making over the past ten years) so she could lend her skills to making it legible and more user friendly.

A big thanks to Manfred Lemke, another passionate home bread producer introduced to me by Jonquil. Manfred dispelled many of the off-putting stories I had heard about the publishing world, making it possible for a unknown person such as myself with something to say, to publish and market their beliefs.

Thank you all

Clive Mellum

"Clive is the most knowledgeable and generous person I have met in the industry."

Laura Hart, Harts Bakery, Bristol

Contents

Introduction

How it all began

This may well be a long introduction to my book but I tell you all this to gain your trust in its practical content. It's not just a book of recipes for inspiration as so many modern books can be, it is a book of techniques on how to use the limited ingredients we have to work with, to help you to gain control of the science involved in manufacturing these basic foods. There are few pictures and more facts. Some of the terminology may be difficult to understand if you are just starting out, so it will be simplified as we travel along together. I want to encourage you to continue practising, so you gain the confidence to use the terminology historically used throughout the trade in this country when applying controlled fermentation. Some other parts may well justify a more in-depth complex explanation for the more advanced, but this can sometimes be rather daunting for the beginner, so won't be included. I hope to help a wider audience to benefit from my life's work. There will be many procedures to adhere to, almost to the point of being over the top, but they will all be relevant to problems regularly encountered through my career of problem-solving at all levels of baking. Some problems have been raised in the many emails I receive, or in-house from the very large to the very small bakeries where I have been invited to help. You may get away with leaving some of the terminology out, but if I leave too many terms out, there will come a time when the flour can't cope, causing it to give up, and you won't understand why. This won't be the fault of the mill but a lack of implementing the controls necessary to complement the flour.

Over the many years I have been involved with the baking industry, I have been lucky enough to be able to help many different people in many different places in many different ways. I have shown them how an understanding of the basic laws of fermentation will complement their skills. The aspiring bakers span the whole range, from the up-and-coming wanting to be famous, to the already rich and famous. I have worked with the Queen's chefs, with lords, also in princes' kitchens; with people who bake for therapy, some out of necessity with dietary problems; from big and expensive kitchens hardly ever used for cooking for a family, to small kitchens with one bread machine and many mouths to feed; from bakers five years of age to as old as eighty-seven. They all had something in common. They wanted to understand the reason why their breads can be good one day and then totally different the next.

I've worked in very large bakeries with no other interest than the bottom line profit margin, and in small bakeries run by passionate souls whose sole aim is to produce the best product they can for their friends and customers, gaining their rewards purely from the pleasure they give with this basic food.

A great number of special people have stuck in my mind whom I feel privileged to have worked with. Many of them entered the trade with little or no training. There were very few places to gain this experience from the 1980s onward, as the industry had become de-skilled over the years. As with so many other producers of valued food in this country, they had become driven purely by the desire to drop out of their existing jobs on the nine-to-five treadmill for the small rewards thrown to them by the very people who relied on them to secure their own jobs at the top. Many people had been forced to fill in their time at home after becoming unemployed as company profit became a higher priority than the welfare of these unfortunate people and their families. They chose to do this – to follow their hearts rather than their pockets – and yes, you can make money from hands-on baking, but only if you have the passion and you are prepared to work long and unsociable hours to achieve it. There are only so many loaves that can be made with one man's passion, and this becomes diluted as small bakeries grow and expand, employing more people to cope, sometimes having to compromise their beliefs to cope with the demand. Baking is a disease that eats away at you as you strive for perfection; you curse it when you are in it as it can be so frustrating. But your mind will continually be brought back to it when you are away from it. Only those who have experienced this will understand.

Through supporting the independent flour milling industry over the past thirty-four years, I have travelled more than two million miles throughout the British Isles and parts of Europe, taking every opportunity to encourage people not only to work with traditional flours to complement their products, but also to enhance them with controlled fermentation of some form, rather than the quick-fix Chorleywood process using dough enhancers as a substitute. This modern method has evolved over the years and become more complex as food technologists gathered more knowledge of enzyme activity and how to apply it to our daily bread to eliminate the need for fermentation. Adding this concoction to breads will make the small bakers' breads no different from most breads you will find on the supermarket shelf, hence the demise of the independent baker through the bleak days of the 80s and 90s. It has been a fascinating journey for me, playing a very small part in the resurrection of this skill, as for many years we had been encouraged to eat products produced for speed and profit rather than enjoyment.

Many people and circumstances have influenced this re-birth, and probably travel has had the biggest influence since the 80s. As we travelled we found an enjoyment in eating some of the breads available in other countries, so on returning home we would continually be searching for something with a similar shape. Unfortunately, even if you could find it on the shelf, the same trickery had been applied in most cases, with little respect for the flavour, texture or even digestion. Every opportunity I had on my holidays abroad, and later while developing flours and customer relationships for the independent millers, I would bake with these skilled Europeans, as there was very little opportunity to extend my knowledge in this country. Over many years of working with them, I came to respect their values and skills, but sadly now they are quickly changing their way of life, and unfortunately they are heading off down the same sorry slippery road as this country did some seventy-plus years ago. So much so that on my return from my last eight-week baking tour around Europe I felt proud of what has evolved in this country over the past thirty years. Although we still have a long way to go, we have turned the corner, raising the quality of many of our basic foods and drinks. This has been driven mainly by the general public's desire to understand the foods they eat.

Once again our up-and-coming small producers are starting to gain a foothold as people begin to appreciate quality, but this will carry a cost; if a product is under-priced there will be short cuts applied to producing it. If the right price is paid for something as basic as breads, then investment can be made in educating our up-and-coming passionate bakers who have chosen this hard way of life. If the education is there, we can only carry on evolving for the better, hopefully getting back to every village having a quality baker who appreciates their importance to the food chain, and every county having an independent miller to support and complement this skill, as we would have had historically.

My grandfather and great-grandfather, and indeed my uncle, were all bakers who knew their trade and I have often referred to their historical books for inspiration or problem-solving, especially when I started to promote organic products. Their skills were passed down from generation to generation, and they knew the importance of the handful of ingredients they had to work with in those days, also when to apply them to obtain the control of the eating quality as well as the texture they desired.

My father was brought up on a farm but did try to be a baker through the difficult years after the war, then sensibly followed his heart and went back to his love of being a farm worker; this strangely was the reason for me starting out along this interesting road. The farm he had chosen to work on, unfortunately for me in those days, was up a small lane some one and a half miles long, so at the age of eleven the only way for me to get to public transport was to walk or suffer the humiliation of being dropped off or picked up in the milk lorry or on the tractor or what would be classed as a less-than-legal van nowadays. I became tired of this daily embarrassment so requested a bike; quite rightly, my parents told me that money didn't grow on trees. This was a valuable first lesson and one I would become grateful to them for all through my life.

Dad came back one day to inform me he had found me a bike made up from bits and pieces from the local bike shop. This would cost me twelve pounds ten shillings (Wow, thanks Dad!). "I have also found you a job you can do after school so you can pay me back", he said. (Not what I expected.) This job just happened to be in the local bakery some three miles from the bottom of the lane; on reflection this wasn't such a bad option, as the very thing I disliked about farming was the cold winters and this job conjured up thoughts of being in a nice warm environment through the chilly months. Lesson number two was quickly learnt. The bakery was then still baking in what was called a faggot oven; this was fired by wood, so through the winter months I had to work out in the cold to coppice the hazel thickets, bundling the stems into tight faggots ready to cram into the oven for energy. The upside was on a Saturday; I was allowed to go into the bakery to work with the big boy greasing the tins and prepping for the next week's production. This was where the fascination started and I first became infected at such an early age with a passion for this rewarding industry.

At the age of fourteen and now on my second drop-handlebar racing bike, unfortunately still made up from second hand bits and pieces, I showed potential, so was offered a baking apprenticeship with the grand wage of three pounds fifteen shillings a week minus my college and book fees. My school teachers strongly advised me to take this opportunity as my track record at school had never been that good. I was allowed to leave early as the bakery was short staffed through the Easter rush.

The apprenticeship was one of the last in this country and was designed to give you practical experience five days a week in the bakery, then one day a week travel to a technical college to gain both theory and practical skills. This was to take two years to obtain the basic City and Guilds qualification, then a further two years to obtain the advanced City and Guilds, then a further two years of evening classes in your own time after a day's work to obtain the Nationals and Higher Nationals. By now travel wasn't a problem, as I had two wheels with an engine, but not the fast two-fifty motorbike I had dreamt of so I could become a Rocker like the other boys in the bakery. Instead I had to suffer their banter about becoming a Mod as my disposable income had become a problem and I was given this eighteen-year-old rather shabby Lambretta scooter by a generous relative, but it had potential and it was all in a good cause.

The apprenticeship on its own was a wonderful education and fired my enthusiasm on a weekly basis; the added advantage was working with a passionate Austrian baker, who came over to this country in the 1920s, bringing his baking skills with him. He was strict and firm, with a quiet way of instilling his love of this science into me to achieve the daily high standard he expected from his products and the people working for him. I didn't fully appreciate the importance of this man and his knowledge in my life until my mid-thirties, and will be eternally grateful to him for his encouragement. I easily achieved good results at college, as this industry was known to be practical and hands-on, so the exam results were marked on the content of your written exams rather than the way it was put down on paper, which was a bit of an advantage for me. Contrary to my headmaster's belief, I did have the capability of storing information; I just had difficulty in translating this onto paper.

At the age of twenty-one I was off to sleepy Dorset with my little family to run my own bakery, with a dream of conquering the world with my new-found skills and be-coming a millionaire by the age of fifty. I would make the bread through the night, put it into the vans in the morning and then drive around the surrounding villages, delivering door to door. Not quite the horse and cart days but close; it was the dream. Sadly through the 1970s our way of life in this country was being influenced great-ly by the supermarket and its convenience foods, and it soon became apparent that sliced breads were taking hold as more and more people requested the soft and pappy breads through the week, occasionally giving themselves a treat with a crusty loaf over the weekend. To try to combat this, a company was set up in Bristol by independent bakers to mass-produce breads made with the Chorleywood process; these were then distributed to the small independent baker on a daily basis to try to help them survive. Although this did help, seven years on with two shops and four rounds, a high percent-age of my production was bought in to feed this demand. Yes, we could make money but it became frustrating and pointless to have the traditional knowledge and training and not to use it. I just wanted to make breads to be proud of; sadly the demand for this was slowly to disappear, with little consideration of what was being added to the tasteless mass that was to take over, or the harm it would be doing to us over the years.

I made the decision in 1980, as did so many other small bakers at this time, to close my shops and to pursue a technical career with the bakery suppliers to the industry. These positions were few and far between as the industry became de-skilled, so I settled for selling flour with a small independent miller based in Gloucester to help feed the family and pay the mortgage. By this time the surviving bakeries had also slowly moved to producing their breads with the Chorleywood process, as they had been told by the producers of this magic dust that this was the way forward to save cost and speed production. By doing so they saved on skilled labour; this brought added pressures, as this additive would make their breads just the same as supermarket bread. The speed with which they fell by the wayside increased dramatically and became painful to watch on a weekly basis as I called on them to sell flour.

Unfortunately for the flour industry, when small bakers are being sold magic ingredients with limited knowledge on how to apply them, they think they are the answer to all their problems, so any problems encountered would now be the fault of the flour. Luckily for me the larger flour mills had also decided to dispense with their technical staff to cut costs, so when problems occurred I soon gained credit for helping people out, guiding them through their problems by trying to swing them back to adding some form of concentrated fermentation. This would be done with the simplest of forms, the traditional overnight sponge. Most times it would mainly end up a compromise of still using improvers and just implementing the basic laws of fermentation, development, temperature and hydration to add control and re-balance the product, as the fear of costing them time had set in, and speed seemed to be paramount over quality. To go back to thinking ahead to set ferments seemed an unnecessary burden.

Through the early 1990s my trade had reached an all-time low. We were down to a very small number of independent bakers with uninteresting products, while mass-produced breads were being sold for as little as 17p per 800g loaf. Every trick had been applied to make this bread as cheap as possible, using inferior wheat fortified with added dried glutens, adding bromate to strengthen these glutens and in some cases running the flour over chlorine gas to bleach it to help the miller to work to high extractions. Couple all this with the way the bread improvers had evolved out of control; is it any wonder this decline in craft bakeries took place?

What weren't taken into account were the price-controlling factors involved in producing this underestimated food. The farmer is at the mercy of our weather. He also needs to sow and maintain the grain for many months using expensive equipment and costly labour; some years after a poor harvest he may be required to dry the grain to ensure it reaches the miller with the right moisture specification. This can also be an added cost having to be absorbed. The grain then goes to a grain merchant who stores and distributes the grain under close scrutiny. In some cases we strive for traditional continental breads, and this grain is transported from country to country by road and boat. The miller will have invested many millions of pounds in sophisticated equipment and training personnel to ensure continuity, traceability and consistency in their chosen specifications. This helps to control something that is subject to much variability, as it is a living product. This heavy bulky product should then be stored in large warehouses to condition the flour. A representative is employed to call on the customers to support them, and the orders are processed to the customers' individual requirements by a team of people at head office. Orders are then sent through to the warehouse for picking before loading onto the lorries. Because of many transport restrictions on our busy roads and cities, and customer personnel requirements that need to be taken into account, most of this flour is delivered through the night, adding more cost to ensure an efficient service by the miller to the baker.

When the flour reaches the bakery, even the smallest of bakery set ups will have invested many thousands of pounds in their equipment and training the staff who are working unsociable hours to ensure products with such a short shelf life reach the public as fresh as they possibly can for their enjoyment. After all of this investment throughout this chain, bread still continues to be underestimated for its food value and is indeed under-priced. If it's cheap, something will be missing; this will normally be skill or fermentation. We should be encouraged to look at bread as we do meat: eating a small amount of a good cut of expensive meat presented well can be a real pleasure, unlike a large plateful of something not cared for and cooked beyond recognition.

Another example I always give is beer. When I first started out baking, it would take me an hour's work to purchase a good loaf of bread or a pint of beer that was really enjoyable to drink. With a good plate of bread and cheese, you would only need one pint of this to savour the pleasure. The brewing industry has gone through a similar miserable process of streamlining and adding other ingredients to cut cost and to speed up production, so much so that I stopped drinking it. It ceased to be a pleasure and only made me feel uncomfortable. We now have a rebirth of really good caring micro-breweries popping up throughout the country and I can enjoy this simple pleasure again but it will cost me at least three pounds per pint for this pleasure, just as a loaf of bread should but no one is being paid three pounds an hour! How priorities have changed in one lifetime.

It would seem that all things need to reach a low before they can start to move forward. The organic movement had always been in the background with a strange reputation of being slightly left over from those lovely hippy days I lived through (Man!) but these few producers had beliefs and maintained them through each decade and survived. The opportunity presented itself for me to join a very small independent organic flour mill, once again in the Gloucester region; they were producing just stone ground organic flour but had a dream of promoting this lifestyle, enhancing the environment and people's welfare as a priority, so I joined them to help this cause move forward.

In my mind Organic has been the springboard for the rebirth of our interest in foods and how they are produced. Every time there was a food scare through the 90s there would be a sudden upsurge in product development using organic ingredients, giving me the opportunity to enter many bakeries all over the country to work with them on developing products without any enhancers. Fermentation was to be the only answer; this set many challenges for me and encouraged me to dig deep into my baking skills, giving me many opportunities to challenge my knowledge and work out how to translate it to the production staff as simply as possible to encourage them to follow it.

Organic will always be there and it's a word people trust, but its demise in bread came when the supermarkets started to promote it. Sadly this put pressure on the controlling bodies to approve organic bread improvers or dough enhancers. Yes, there are approved organic ingredients that have strict controls that cost a lot of money to implement, but once again they bypass the very thing that is most important in bread – long fermentation – so organic breads on the shelf can be produced by developing (mixing) for two and a half minutes on a high speed mixer with high hydration, six minutes' intermediate proof, forty minutes' final proof and then a twenty-two minute bake; nothing different then except the word organic.

Organic in bread had now done its job in educating the general public, as they were starting to question the foods they eat and what is in them, so I found myself starting to work with the general public over and above my normal working week, answering many emails and having lengthy phone conversations as people continually mistrusted the foods they were eating. Occasionally I would gather a bunch of like-minded people together in the test bakery at the mill, in kitchens or cookery schools, to dismiss some of the mysteries attached to fermentation. Little did I know this was to become a major part of my life towards the latter part of my working career. This upsurge has been driven and complemented by the sharing of information through television, YouTube, the Internet and glossy recipe books that started to make it look easy, encouraging many people to want to have a go but often their attempts ended in disappointment.

I can't eat bread

As the interest in breads gathered momentum, a common question being asked was, Why do I suffer discomfort when eating it? When you come to analyse it, there is little wonder. Look at the way bread has evolved over the two-plus generations since the middle of the twentieth century, and the path we have been led down with the general public's quest for cheap food. The high profit margins required to build empires and trade names cannot sustain true bread. Many suffer discomfort after eating breads purchased from the supermarket shelves. Of the few people I have been able to work with through email or around the workbench, experimenting with them eating breads with concentrated fermentation added, using softer wheats and ancient grains, and removing dough enhancers, many have been able to find their way back to the pleasures this simple food can bring. Unfortunately there are many true coeliacs for whom this will not work, so be careful.

Recently doctors and the self-diagnosed general public seem keen to put too many people under the coeliac umbrella, causing people problems in searching for very expensive alternatives such as gluten-free breads, which may well have their own consequences seventy years down the road, as food technologists lend their skills to them. If you start by taking bread out of your diet for a few weeks, then start eating 100% rye breads using the Mother dough at high percentages for a few weeks, slowly move forward to making breads using ancient grains with low yeast and long chilled ferments (explained under the spelt recipe later) you may find you are among the many who have travelled this path, ending up able to eat all-white breads with either overnight or simple sponges added. Making your breads at home with knowledge will at least give you control to be able to experiment, to make the breads that suit you and your digestive system, or armed with this information at least search out and support one of our many up-and-coming true bakers who know the reason for adding fermentation to their breads. Don't be timid in asking them their process; if they are genuine they will be proud of their skills and beliefs and want to share them with you. I hope this fact – long fermentation process – will one day be printed on the bag or wrapper rather than the list of enhancers added. Don't eat anything you don't want to eat (you are in control).

Bread has evolved over many thousands of years, some kinds through necessity, some through accidental findings or personal taste. As they have evolved, people have christened them with a name to personalise them, giving them an identity which is great for reference, but as I have travelled and worked with so many different passionate bakers, I find this a little difficult to work with. When it comes to method, every baker will be making the same named product in a totally different way, creating subtle differences in flavour and texture to suit their production with their own beliefs. I have learnt over the years of helping people to look at the product of their choice from a basic ingredient listing: flour, salt, yeast and water. All breads start from this point, then some will choose to make them tighter; some will be slacker with high water absorption; some will ferment longer with lower yeast levels before the add-on ingredients go in, but keeping to the basic building blocks will create a base dough tolerant enough to carry any other additional ingredient you may wish to add through the process. If a dough is not set in a controlled environment, it will be guesswork all the way through from this point on, so some days it may work well and other days you will be disappointed.

As we travel through the book I will be giving you many different pointers that I have discovered over and above my initial apprenticeship. While I strived for perfection in my products, this could almost be to the extent of being over the top but they will all be relevant to problems that I have been asked to help solve over the years. Some of you may well be able to identify with them, and this will help you to improve your skills and understanding of this science. But don't become a slave to the book; that will make your bread-making experience become a chore, making you reluctant to continue this pleasure. Use it as reference by dipping in and out to make your breads in the time you have with the taste, texture and crust you like. If you try to emulate a picture in a recipe book with only half the story, the results might not be what you expect. Always question the list of ingredients and when you need to add them to the process; each of them will be added to enhance the product, so they will all have a job to do, and can change the bread totally if added at the wrong time.

Why Bother To Bake?

To eat and enjoy breads with an aim of achieving perfection, they will need to be controlled all the way through the process. We will be looking to reach optimum fermentation (when the yeasts have converted the maltose sugars) just before the breads are set into the oven; I can't tell you where this is as it will move on a daily basis as it is affected by the atmospheric pressures. If you start out wrong then it will be purely guesswork all the way through. If you start out right by implementing some if not all the basic laws of fermentation, then that final window when the dough reaches its peak will broaden out, giving you more leeway at the end of its life. If a loaf is baked from an under ripe dough (under-fermented) there will be a residue of natural sugars remaining in the dough, creating a dough that will take on excess crust colour with a foxy red appearance, fooling you into thinking the product is baked when it isn't. This crust will not go crispy no matter how many tricks you have read about that you apply. It will always remain rubbery and tough when cool. The final spring in the oven will be restricted because the gases produced haven't had sufficient time to work on the gluten strands, resulting in a pinched loaf with unpredictable oven spring through the bake. In some extreme cases the dough can flow out if free-standing when set (put) into the oven, creating those flat Frisbee-breads as described by so many poor people in their emails.

If a dough is spent (over-fermented) all of the natural sugars have been depleted, making it difficult for the crust to take on any colour when baked. The crust will always appear bland and pale in appearance; even if you increase the oven temperature or bake it for longer, it won't be retrievable. The yeast will have exhausted itself through multiplying too quickly as a result of over-feasting. This will create a fragile cell structure that will fracture when the heat penetrates through the loaf as the final bake takes place, encouraging the cells to burst, releasing their gases and falling back. Once again the loaf will flow during the bake if free-standing, having little or no oven spring. It will also be detrimental to the taste of the finished loaf. This crust will have a tough and rubbery bite to it, and in extreme cases the crumb structure can be dense, with uneven cell structure causing it to be a little unpalatable when eaten.

FACT

All breads are edible, as it is only flour, salt, yeast, water and time incorporated in them, but some bread can take a little longer to eat than others. I can only sow the seeds; you make them grow, and control will help you to achieve this.

All the right ingredients without controls will let you down one day, making it disappointing for you. Implement controls gradually until they become second nature to you, then you can forget about them, giving your mind time to start experimenting to make your breads not mine while learning more every time you touch the dough. I still can fifty years on!

HOW THIS BOOK WORKS

I have been encouraged to set this down on paper in the same format as the workshops by the many letters and emails of thanks I have received from people of every walk of life. This information helped them emerge from the fog of vague information they had accumulated. It was also becoming difficult for me to fulfil the demand for this information one-to-one as I slowly approach the end of my career. I hope it translates as well on paper as it did around a workbench.

Following the format that I have developed for the Basic and Advanced workshops as they evolved through the years, I hope this will help to instil as many different base methods as possible, using a variety of ingredients efficiently as we did in the short time I had to work with people on my courses. This will be followed by some of the recipes regularly requested, also some of my personal old favourites to encourage support for our traditions in this country that have fallen by the wayside.

Overview of Basic and Advanced Workshops: Ingredients, Processes, Equipment

- Description of base ingredients, when to use them and what they do

- Concentrated fermentation and its advantages; reference to overnight ferments, sponges or flying sponges as historically referred to in this country

- Control; weighing accurately in a controlled environment to a set time

- Hydration and its consequences

- Development; when to apply aggressively to gain full advantage of extendable gluten, when to respect the cell structure

- Additions; when to incorporate them to enhance the finished article

- Environment; how to care for the dough through the process

- Proving; advantages of the different stages, when to apply and why

- Baking to a specification

- Keeping quality; what will affect it, how to improve using natural ingredients.

PRODUCTS FOR THE BASIC WORKSHOP
to give an insight into as much of this information as possible:

Basic white dough using sponge and dough

Soda bread working with the low development short process

Enriched doughs working with high fats, sugars and flying sponges

Short crust pastry to take you right to the other end of the
gluten development spectrum.

PRODUCTS FOR THE ADVANCED WORKSHOP

Creating a Mother dough; how to start and maintain her

Setting a Mother dough; blending flour to enhance the process

Rye Breads; how to set and handle them

Open crumb; how to work with high additions of concentrated sponges
and high hydration

Soft crumb; using natural ingredients to produce baps, soft breads and lardy cake
(if you dare)

Scone as an in-between short pastry and bread.

EQUIPMENT NEEDED AT THIS STAGE

the most important is **accurate digital scales** capable of weighing to one gram,
next a **probe thermometer**, a couple of **jugs**, a strong pair of willing **arms** if mixing
by hand, possibly a **scraper** and a good **solid work surface**.

The rest will be added on as we progress; most of them you will already have in
your kitchen.

Ingredients

I always encourage people to work in kilos, grams and percentages for ease of being able to set a recipe with precision at the start. This also helps you to cross check your favourite recipes, making sure they are also in balance, and helping them to conform to the basic laws of fermentation when applied. Don't worry though; I will put both percentages and weights side by side for you to use while you get an understanding of this procedure. Most base doughs are made up of only a handful of the same ingredients. Flour is normally the main ingredient used, so this will always be classed as the 100%. Every other ingredient added will follow through as a percentage of this weight, helping you to weigh and set a dough with accuracy, and eliminating the necessity for having to continually refer to the recipe of your choice. Another advantage is that you can make the recipe any size you want it to be; for instance if your normal recipe uses 500g of flour and you only have 300g left in your bag, there will be no excuse. You can still make a somewhat smaller loaf but in balance. If you have friends coming round and you need to make two loaves, you can quickly multiply your quantity of flour then all the other ingredients will follow through, ensuring the recipe is still in balance.

FLOUR

There are many different flours available nowadays and they will each bring their different characteristic to your breads. As you discover them the temptation will be like entering a sweet shop for the first time as a child; you will want to try them all. It may be better to stick to one flour of your choice to start with while you gain experience in setting and controlling fermentation. When you have perfected the range above, then start to venture out, experimenting with them as add-ons for taste, texture and performance. You will be surprised how the tolerances will change throughout the process and how your new-found skills will need to be applied slightly differently to each flour.

All flours are manageable as long as you know their specification before you start using them. They all have a percentage of functional gluten, starches and natural sugars within them. Each one of these plays an important part in the process. Doing a gluten wash can help you to identify a particular flour's specification and its characteristics. Choose a good quality white flour from a reputable miller. Place just 50g of this into a bowl, add 30g of cold water and bring this to a small dough ball, making sure it is fully developed. Once mixed, wash away all the sugars and starches by manipulating under a gently running tap. This will eventually leave you with just the functional gluten. Once washed, place into a hot oven and watch as it leaps into action, expanding to form a big blister. If the gluten is suspect in any way this will not happen, or the blister will fracture and fall back as it expands. The quality of this part of flour is critical to forming a good cell structure. As fermentation starts to produce gases, these need to be retained within the cell they create for as long as possible to do their job. The downside of this rubbery-textured product is that if this hasn't had a long fermentation time, as with the breads using dough enhancers or improvers, then it will be down to your body to digest this, causing many different digestive problems as it passes through your system. I have had many lovely letters over the years from people finding their way back to eating real breads just by appreciating this fact and making small changes to the breads they choose to eat and where they buy them from, or simply making them themselves.

Some grains such as the ancient bearded grains, Spelt for example, haven't been engineered in any way so will have different properties within them. Because of this they are gaining a reputation for being easier to digest but these flours still contain a percentage of functional glutens that will benefit from being fermented to help the digestion even more.

FLOURS USED

White flour for demonstration purposes: when implementing fermentation, I prefer to use a flour produced using predominantly 80% of our UK wheat incorporated into the miller's grist (blend of wheats); this will bring those lovely natural sweet flavours to the breads. The remaining 20% will be made up of the harder wheats grown in the warmer countries; this will add the tolerance needed through the longer ferments. When you first start out experimenting with concentrated fermentation, the addition of these harder wheats will have very little impact on the base flour flavours within them, other than helping to retain the fermentation when added. The myth that has evolved throughout the baking industry as our skills disappeared is that the more of these harder wheats used, the better the flour will be. This may well bring body and profitable hydration to the cell structure in a short process relying on dough enhancers, but not so in my opinion with long ferments. It can and will work against you when controlled fermentation is not being practiced efficiently, causing them to pinch back at the very time they should be springing into action, as the heat penetrates through the dough in the baking process and the yeast spores are having their last little flurry before the heat kills them off.

It is also very costly shipping this grain around the world using precious resources to do so. Why import grain? Let us feed ourselves with our own grain as much as possible and in doing so, support our ailing farming industry while continuing to develop our own baking skills to complement our own grains. It must be remembered that it is a three-way partnership between the farmer, the miller and the baker. All flours are manageable if we don't expect the breads to be a uniform shape and keep for a month; breads are designed to be passed around, eaten and enjoyed, with love and respect for the effort and skill lent by the person producing them. Using a softer flour and practising balance and control to enhance it is a better option for flavour, palate, texture and digestion.

Every harvest grown in this county will naturally fluctuate as it is so reliant on our changeable weather. Unfortunately despite every effort and the controls practiced throughout what is now a very skilled independent milling industry, there will always be an element of the unknown for the first few months of a new crop. This may start to filter through to you from late September through to the end of November but it will start to settle down as the grain becomes aged. This is attributed to the fact that it is a living product and small variations will appear, changing its characteristics.

So, as with the miller at this time of year, your baking skills will now need to be questioned, encouraging you to go back to basics to eliminate any bad habits you may have implemented through the previous year, as your confidence grows and complacency creeps in with the continuity of the flour of the previous year. An average white flour for a free-standing loaf will demand 60% to 62% water and 62% to 64% for a tin loaf. The open crumb demands much higher volumes, and for some can be as high as 95%, but technique needs to be practised to help them carry this higher quantity. This will be explained later for the open-crumbed products. Hydration within the doughs is paramount for the finished quality of your chosen breads. All of these water absorptions may sometimes fluctuate slightly from delivery to delivery so you will need to use discretion through the early development stages. This is done by feeling and stretching to ensure the consistency is correct. Some higher protein or stronger flours demand higher water absorptions, some softer or lower proteins demand less. Too tight a dough will restrict a balanced fermentation, creating an under ripe dough (under-fermented) in the set time allocated, causing dough to flow. Too wet and the dough will also flow if more fermentation time and folds are not added to compensate for this.

Rye flour has a very small percentage of this gluten and can be as low as 0.6% as opposed to the 40% plus found within a good quality white flour. Making rye breads is a good place to start if you do have difficulties enjoying breads. There are predominantly three different ones readily available now in this country, a very light, a medium and a dark, all relating to the bran content. The very light is used for cake and addition to white flours, up to 50% of the recipe for eastern European breads. It can be used as a natural enhancer or help with oven burst when using high protein flours. The medium is normally used as the base for breads produced with 100% rye flour. The dark is used for adding colour and texture to the darker pumpernickel-type breads. I also often use this product at small percentages as a crumb softener, a dough relaxant and a flavour enhancer, as you will see as we progress through the book. It can be used as 100% of your flour base, but because of its makeup being high in starch and having a lack of functional gluten, this will need a different approach when mixing and handling (it can get a bit messy).

Rye is an under-estimated flour, and luckily for me being educated by an Austrian baker, it was a big part of my early education in my range of breads. Unfortunately I had some bad experiences of people not understanding this bread and its importance when I first moved to my bakery in Dorset. These wonderful breads through the early seventies quickly became eradicated from our diet in the public's quest for soft long-life sliced convenient cheap breads.

This flour demands much higher hydration than white, and because it can be added in so many different levels to many different products, it is difficult to give you its average water absorption. If you look at it as being added to a product as an additional flour or as 100% of the yeasted product, then I would normally allow for about 95% hydration for a medium rye flour. Traditionally these breads should be produced using the sourdough culture. This was one of the problems in promoting this product: as traditions became forgotten, as soon as you said the word 'sour' people would take a step back. Then if you could get them to taste it, before the flavour even registered on the palate they would be screwing their noses up only to reject it as being undesirable, or words to that effect in rural farmworkers' language. As I progressed, trying to invent ways to encourage this taste, it slowly occurred to me that people would start to respect it more readily if you dispensed with the word 'sour' and replaced it with the logic that this base brew is continually refreshed daily, ready to give birth to all the other doughs made with it. It slowly became christened Mother dough. Most people love their Mums, helping them to warm to this bread more readily. Later it was to become an asset when teaching, causing a lot of humour while helping people to understand and remember.

This reminds me of a wonderful story of a man of the cloth who attended the workshop. As with everybody at the end of our day together, he went off with a small amount of both the rye and white Mother to encourage the bakers to look after her and possibly make bread with her. As with so many, after a few weeks I received an email from him, giving me an update on his progress. In it he said that the white Mother was fine, bubbling away and making breads regularly, but the rye was giving him so much grief he might have to christen her the Mother-in-law! Sorry, I digress.

This culture will then need to be added at very high percentages for the acidity and basic yeast spores within it. The controlled acidity will help to gel these starches as the breads bake. While the basic yeast spores ferment to create gas retained in this gel, the water absorption within the base flour when applied to the main recipe will be at the mercy of the consistency and quantity of this culture you add. If you work with a Mother dough with a thick creamy batter consistency as suggested later, using a medium rye, then 80% hydration will be a good guide. I have found little advantage to fermenting the full dough for long periods of time, so prefer to give the care and attention to the Mother dough I add; this will help to process the dough relatively quickly through the final stage.

Whole-wheat flour can sometimes wrongly be referred to as wholemeal; it should be just be the whole of the wheat berry simply conditioned to the right moisture content before it hits the mill. To my mind, it should also be traditionally milled on stones to obtain its full nutritional benefits. The best flavours come from using the softer wheat such as our own wheats grown in this country, but it can be less forgiving through production, as all the bran is incorporated, reducing the amount of functional gluten dramatically. This bran can also be sharp, so it can start to break down the functional gluten as development takes place, so it's worth folding in all of the allocated water to the flour before adding any of the other ingredients. Just give this, say, fifteen or twenty minutes to hydrate to help release any endosperm (or white flour particles still clinging to the bran). This will also help make this bran become supple, helping to prevent a breakdown happening as you stretch and tear the dough. These flours have lots of roughage in them with wonderful flavours of their own, so they benefit from the shorter ferments using the flying sponge or overnight sponges at a small percentage rather than 100% long overnight ferments. The bran content in this product is high, so the water absorption needs to be increased by 10% to 12% compared to white flour. It's worth using your discretion to make the dough as slack as you can handle it at the start, as the bran will slowly carry on taking the moistures on board through the process. If it's too tight when setting (mixing) the dough, this can cause the product to pinch back through the baking process.

You will find many different wholemeals on the shelf; most of them are produced on steel rollers with a high percentage of the hard wheats added, or in some of the lower-priced, gluten. This helps to build in extra tolerances. In some cases with the modern flours the miller has the technology and the equipment to divide the different particles of the berry off so that they can be re-blended to a specific specification before bagging off. This can mean that there are many variations when changing your flour, so the same discretion will need to be applied to these, even more so than with the white flours. Your skill needs to be practiced when changing any of your chosen flour types.

These are the only flours needed for the full range produced on both the basic and advanced breads. This is done deliberately to help you appreciate the impact the other controls and ingredients will have on your process, thus not being influenced by the changes in performance different flours will bring to the finished article when you use them. As soon as you inject a different flour into the equation, then it becomes difficult to ascertain if it is the elements or the nature of the flour that is making the difference, so while learning it is advisable to confine your production to a small range of flours.

Flour is a living product, so can and will vary from harvest to harvest despite all the heavy investment by the miller to eliminate variations. When you add something live to the doughs in the form of yeast, flours become susceptible to the influences of such things as atmospheric pressure, humidity and ambient temperature. These are factors you cannot change in your baking environment so they can make it very difficult to control, making it more important to implement the other controls we will be working with to help with consistency.

Having said all this, if you have a product that you make regularly and you are proud of it, please don't change this. Just add some of the controls we cover to help you move forward and be more adventurous in your bread making. Bread is very personal and I have learnt never to judge bread, as other people's opinions of what gives pleasure to one may be unacceptable to another. I didn't invent bread; I have just learnt to work with it. When you have perfected something and you have confidence in it, pass this information on to keep this industry moving forward, ensuring we never return to the bleak days of the 80s and 90s. Bread should not be confined to the sandwich; it should be passed around the table with every meal. It can also give great pleasure to many people to receive it as a gift, knowing you have taken the trouble to use your time and energy in making this simple present. I can only sow the seeds for you, so you will be the one to make them grow. Gradually as you become affected by this art, you should naturally start criticising the finished article, continually wanting to improve on it. This is good and will encourage you to learn something different about it each time you touch it. I can still learn with the same products I have made many many times, fifty years from the first time I ever touched it.

One of the big turning points for our breads in this country was when an article appeared in a national newspaper in the 90s, saying that a loaf that was then being imported from France, produced using traditional sour dough fermentation, was being sold through Harrods of London for £9.95. Shock horror! Sliced bread was only 17 pence a loaf. It soon became apparent that people were showing a great deal of interest in this product; many who could afford it were taking it to dinner parties as a gift instead of expensive wines. This certainly helped to open the flood gates, encouraging bakers and the general public to start researching this ancient art that had been so easily dismissed for a generation in this country. This was to become the next busy time for me on product development, just as it was when organic products came into demand with each food scare whipped up by the media. Luckily enough, this momentum has carried on with bread, resulting in my industry continuing to move forward in skills year on year. Thanks to all those responsible and brave enough to have taken the leap forward!

YEAST

There are a few yeasts readily available. The most common and convenient to use are the dried yeasts but be warned: if they have the title of 'fast acting' or 'easy bake dried yeast', they are just that. Look at the ingredient listing; they will have bread improvers added cunningly, disguised as flour treatment agents or dough enhancers. These may well be fine in bread makers or if you choose to make breads on a short process. They are designed to perform within a two-hour programme and the dough will start to deteriorate quickly after this allocated time, so will definitely work against you if you start to extend the fermentation process.

Look for a product labelled 'dried active yeast'. This is the better one to use but unfortunately it comes as encapsulated beads, so whenever you are using them you will need to activate them in a flying sponge condition to ensure the yeast becomes activated and starts multiplying before adding it to the main dough. If you put it straight in you will be chasing these small beads around for ages while they dissolve, putting your dough on the back foot straight away.

On the tin they suggest you stir them with a spoonful of sugar and a little water to help them to activate; to me this is a no-no. I only use purified sugar as a flavouring in an enriched dough. If you introduce purified sugars directly to yeast, yes, they will get excited and froth up but they are different sugars from the maltose sugars within flour, and there are more than enough of these sugars readily available for the yeast to feast on as it reproduces readily before being introduced to the main dough. Use flour instead. Using purified sugar, there will be a rest period while they look for more of the easy sugars, creating a delay in the main dough's activity. It's worth trying one with sugar and one without to satisfy your own curiosity.

ACTIVATING YEASTS

A flying sponge should be used to help you to dip your toe into the most basic form of fermentation. This will be explained in more depth when we come to make the enriched dough in the Basic range, and the soft bap in the Advanced. It consists of setting down a chosen percentage of your flour with all of your yeast, then enough of the total water content allocated to the whole of the recipe to make this amount of flour into a creamy batter consistency. It will need to be tight enough to form a cell (bubble) as fermentation starts but not so tight that it restricts this growth, having a tendency to suffocate rather than cultivate. It should not be so slack (runny) that the cell structure fractures prematurely, losing these precious gases before they can do their work on the cell wall. Precise measurements will be given in the recipes using this method, but the consistency will be the controlling factor rather than the quantity. These dried yeasts, if cultivated this way, can then be used in all breads consistently, even those made in bread machines, contrary to what it says on the manufacturer's tin.

This batter is then given an allocated amount of time to ferment to the maximum. This can be recognised by what is termed falling back, when the yeast cell has reached its maximum extensibility (size), causing it to fracture and fall back naturally, to re-introduce itself to fresh foods to feed on. Normally about forty minutes will be sufficient. To appreciate the importance of this procedure you will benefit from beating this together with your hands, as touch and feel will become a major part of your baking skills. In doing this you will feel the texture and viscosity in this batter at the first stages of its life, then repeat after it has fallen back. It will feel more resilient, giving valuable strength to this small part of the functional gluten in the flour. Also take note of the size of the cell structure before you knock back (expel the gas) and then again after you have knocked back. You will see what was once one big cell has now become hundreds of small cells. Each one of these cells will now have its own yeast spore within, raring to go when introduced to the main part of the dough. This is how we encourage yeasts to multiply, ready for introduction to the other ingredients. Once this momentum is under way you are past first base and it will be very difficult to stop this chain reaction from carrying on.

USAGE

When reading recipes that are set using fresh yeast and you wish to use dried yeast, you will see that the level suggested by the manufacturer will normally be half the weight of dried to fresh, but in reality, under controlled conditions in the test bakery laboratory, it will be more like two thirds. For instance, if the recipe calls for, say, 9g of fresh yeast, I will use 6g of the encapsulated active dried yeast and practise flying sponges to get them to perform in the same window.

FRESH BREWER'S YEAST

Fresh brewer's yeast is commonly used throughout the baking industry. It has evolved from the brewing industry, although it is far removed from the original, as technology has been applied to it to make it more efficient and user friendly. In the industry there is a full range available to help cope with all different scenarios through production. It has become popular as it is very convenient and easy to maintain; it just needs to be refrigerated to keep it cool. The down side of it is that it has a short shelf life and will start to deteriorate after four weeks or even sooner if not kept in an airtight container in the fridge and the fridge isn't running at around 4°C to 5°C. This product is now becoming more readily available; I have seen it appearing in some supermarket chiller cabinets in the UK, just as it is on the continent, in two individual 25g packs. I have found it, bizarrely, with the fresh cream cakes in the past, so you may well have to search for it.

Historically you could go to their in-store bakeries to ask for some and very often they would give it free but recently many people have been saying that they are refusing to offer this service now, on the grounds that it is a living organism, so it is restricted under the Health and Safety laws. Probably this has more to do with the fact that a lot of their bakeries are now using so-called part-bake products rather than manufacturing from base ingredients.

You can readily purchase the product through the Internet but be warned it will definitely be over-priced and can reach you in very poor condition, as the quality will be dependent on how long they have been storing it and how long it takes before you receive it. It may be better to find your local friendly baker to ask if you can purchase some from him. These types of fresh yeast can be added straight into dry ingredients if the right precautions are applied (this will be explained under the heading of salt) or set in the flying sponge condition, depending on the type of product you choose to make. The fresh and dried yeasts are available in an organic version but these are not comfortable being introduced directly to the main ingredients, and it will definitely benefit the finished article if it is set in the flying sponge condition before proceeding to the development stage. Once again I have received many emails on this point.

MOTHER DOUGH YEAST

This is one of the most basic natural yeasts historically used to make breads, and indeed many other foods, for its benefits to our health. When interest in it was first rekindled through the 1990s, unfortunately the Continent was given all the credit; maybe rightly so, as they had continued to practise this art, being conscious of the quality of the foods they ate. But as this was once the only way of making quality breads, our bakers would have been making breads equally as good in the past. It's just that we chose to forget this in our quest for speed and cost. I have come across many different suggestions and personal beliefs over the years as this art has become increasingly popular. I have tried many of them out of curiosity and found some of them to be over complicated, so I always find myself going back to the original way I was first taught through the 1960s.

Once again, if you have achieved starting and maintaining your own Mother Dough that you enjoy working with, please don't change it. This is a very good achievement regardless of how you got there. Just consider some of the logic that follows if you are experiencing any difficulties. Some Mothers on the Continent, as well as throughout the world, will be many years old. Indeed the one I took with me down to Dorset, and which, sadly, I threw away when I closed the bakery, was of a third generation with a lovely story attached to it. I genuinely thought it was the end of my industry and would never be needed again. The ones I have running now are about twenty-two years old and I'm not sure of the significance of this, other than that they now have their own history and have been passed around to many hundreds of people to encourage them to continue passing them on. They can be very unstable for the first three months of starting them off but after this very little will change, providing you service and maintain them properly. The Mother can be made from any flour; she's not fussy, she just wants food to feed off. I have many different ones that I have started over the years to help with product development. They are kept frozen down so that I can resurrect them when needed. For demonstration purposes I just carry a white and a rye Mother. Both of these can be used with most flours as your yeast source, but the rye Mother can be added to many different doughs for taste and texture, and also helps with the keeping quality if added at low percentage. It can also be used to complement a dough produced using fresh or dried yeast rather than sponges or flying sponges, as with pizza or flat breads. People now having educated themselves to eat rye for its digestive advantages, 100% rye breads are becoming more acceptable. Making these breads will demand a high percentage of the rye Mother to be added.

When starting out setting your Mother with the flour of your choice, it is worth considering the darker flours such as wholemeal and dark ryes. These will increase the activity naturally, creating a deeper flavour. The consistency will also change through the first few hours of being fed as the brans hydrate, so always set them slightly slacker at the start. If the consistency tightens, this will also add to this depth of flavour, sometimes making it unpalatable to the newcomer to this type of bread.

There are many fascinating stories of how people entice their wild yeasts to their Mother and I am in no position to dismiss any of them as I haven't tried some of them. This may be a new project for me now I am entering retirement. For now I will pass on to you what I was taught in the bakery all those years ago. Most of these basic spores will come from the outside of wheat berry itself, just as happens on the grape when wine making. If you look closely at the grape or the wheat berry you will see a fine dust that has settled on the outside. These are the spores we use to make our breads and wine. This dust will fall off through the milling process and be incorporated into the flour, so flour without the bran incorporated will still have these valuable spores in it but the darker flours with high bran content will have more, hence the higher activity.

To start this basic activity off will take about five days of continually feeding with just flour and water every twenty-four hours to a set consistency, so be warned: start off really small as it will continually be growing in size as you add more flour and water each day. Every flour will take a different water absorption so I would advise you get into the habit of feeding the Mother to a certain consistency, then you can use any flour you want rather than me giving specific amounts of water to a whole list of flours. I have found the creamy batter consistency will be the best way to describe this, so if I use a standard white flour for the example, then for every 100% flour you use, it will be 125% water added. For example, 100g of flour to 125g of water, but the rye and wholemeal will certainly demand more. The consistency will need to be strong enough to retain the gases for as long as possible when they start to activate, but if it is too tight you will restrict this growth, making them become more acidic to the taste. Through the early days of trying to educate people's palate to this taste, I learnt to keep the Mother mellow in flavour, to encourage people to want to eat it. Maintaining her at a pH of about 3.5 to 4 would give me this. Her consistency will be the controlling factor; please don't rush out to buy a pH meter, it won't be necessary. It's just a way to emphasise the importance of this fact. Nowadays I get youngsters saying, "You won't make one strong enough in taste for me. I love it just as I did with the curries through the seventies", and this is so encouraging. If this is the case, just run the Mother tighter; feeding her less frequently will help.

TO START A MOTHER DOUGH

DAY ONE	%	GRAMS
White flour	100	50
Warm water	125	62-63

With your hand beat to a creamy batter and take note of the consistency; eventually with practice you will be able to feed the Mother without weighing the ingredients. Cover with something other than cling film to avoid skinning and place in the corner of the kitchen for twenty four hours.

DAY TWO: ADD	%	GRAMS
White flour	100	25
Warm water	125	31-32

Each time beat together with your hand or fingertips rather than a utensil to feel the change in the viscosity.

DAY THREE: ADD	%	GRAMS
White flour	100	30
Warm water	125	37-38

DAY FOUR: ADD	%	GRAMS
White flour	100	35
Warm water	125	43-44

DAY FIVE: ADD	%	GRAMS
White flour	100	40
Warm water	125	50

DAY SIX

You will now have just over 400g of Mother bubbling away in the tub, so you can see how quickly it builds up; it is as well to make sure the tub is large enough when you start out to allow for this growth, bearing in mind on a good day she can increase in size as she gets excited after she has been fed. This volume can increase her size by one third as fermentation takes place but she will settle down and find a level after the initial surge, so ensure she has sufficient room to do so to prevent her spewing over the work top.

She is now ready to use as yeast; the uses and methods will be explained in full when we come to using her later on in the advanced stage.

RYE MOTHER

For the rye Mother you will need to follow the above procedures but the water content will need to be at the higher rate of 200% of the flour content. Example: 50g of medium ash [see Appendix] rye flour to 100g of warm water. The next day 25g of flour to 50g of warm water and so on.

STORAGE CONTAINERS

At all times she needs to be kept in a container large enough to cope with the volume and growth but with a lid that can pop when she becomes active, or just a plastic bag over the top will be sufficient. It is only to retain the moistures given off; this will prevent the mixture from skinning up. Never lock her into a vessel such as a Kilner jar or screw top or lock-tight tub unless transporting, as she needs oxygen to breathe. She can suffocate if starved of it for long periods. If she is running at an ambient temperature she will have different amounts of activity each day, as she is affected by many natural elements that we as bakers have no control over, so some days she will increase in volume more than others but will always find a level and tick along after this initial burst.

CARING FOR MOTHER

Don't be a slave to her; keep it simple. If you use her every day she will need to be fed at least 30% of her weight in fresh flour every twenty-four hours to keep her alive and healthy. If you fall below this figure the tendency will be for her to slowly start to become sluggish. If this practice continues, eventually she will cease to be active as the acidity's build-up overcomes the fresh spores each time flour is added. You can't seem to over-feed them but at the same time you don't to want to breed a monster. As there are only so many friends that you can pass it on to, keep her to the size required for your production needs, adding a generous 30% of her weight in fresh flour plus the necessary water addition to keep that creamy batter consistency she likes. When she is up and running at an ambient temperature I always add just cold water from the tap (I've tried all the distilled water and many other suggestions and didn't find them to be a priority in fault-finding, also not practical when large volumes are to be achieved).

Once she has been fed, look on it as having a twenty-four-hour window in which to set (make) your doughs. During the first twelve hours she will need to reach a peak, through the second twelve-hour period she will be hungry and searching for fresh foods to feast on, so anywhere within this second twelve hours will be the ideal time to use her to set your doughs. Once used, she will need to be refreshed ready for the next production run. This could be any time after the next twelve hours but before the twenty-four and so on.

If you only want to make bread, say, once a week, then as soon as you have finished using her, just keep her covered to avoid skinning and pop her in the fridge without feeding. Providing your fridge is running at between 4°C to 5°C nothing much will happen. If it ventures higher there is a danger that she could start to deteriorate. I have kept them in this state of limbo for as long as four weeks without feeding but it may be as well to limit this practice to a week when starting out so you don't add any complication. Mother can be a little temperamental through the first three or four months of her life and may object to being treated like this so early in her life. When you want to use her, bring her out and give her a generous feed, just above the minimum 30% of fresh flour and enough warm water to make the creamy batter. The warm water will help her to recover more quickly; she will then be ready and raring to help you make your breads twelve hours later.

If you only want to make breads, say, once a month or you are lucky enough to go away on holiday for a month at a time, don't burden the neighbour or friend with the responsibility feeding her. This has been known to ruin many a good friendship. Put her into the freezer. Yes, doing this will kill the yeast spores, as will freezing any yeast in my experience, but it will suspend all the other important elements within her such as bacteria and acidity. When you want to resurrect her, bring her out, let her recover naturally at room temperature for twenty-four hours, then feed with flour and warm water as above. Twelve hours after this she should have kicked in. Sometimes through the winter months, if your house is particularly cold, you may need to stand the container somewhere warm; not directly on a radiator or over the cooker but within close vicinity to capture some of the heat. The other option would be to feed twice through the twelve hours, helping to multiply these basic yeast spores, giving her the kiss of life she may well need to get going again.

OVER PRODUCTION OF MOTHER

Don't limit yourself to using it just as a yeast for your breads. As I travelled through Eastern Europe I saw them use it as a meat tenderiser by marinating their meats overnight before they barbeque them. Try it with the rye; it should give a lovely crisp coat on the outside and tender meat on the inside that will melt in your mouth. I have used it as a thickener for gravy; add it to your steak pies instead of ale scrumpy; with the white just add a pinch of salt and a teaspoon of sugar to three generous tablespoons of Mother, mix it well together then drop it onto a hot plate just as you would with a scotch pancake. This is something regularly practised by my many grandchildren, although I must say every now and then there is a tendency for them to get the sugar ratio wrong, ending in it closely resembling a brandy snap, but what will it matter? It's encouraging them to work with their food and see how it can change appearance with different ingredients.

YEAST ADDITION

When using all of the above yeasts they will all need to be added at different levels according to the time you allocate to your chosen process. A shorter process will demand more, a longer process less, regardless of the type, but be careful especially on a short process, as if you go too high you will have residues of yeasts not being depleted through the process, resulting in a very over-powering taste and aroma of yeast in the finished article. In some cases of plant (mass produced) breads, when yeasts are used as a dynamite to blow a bubble in the rubber rather than as a fermentation aid, the effect can be excessively high, leaving residues after baking that can aggravate the gut. This will also often be the case in recipes when using bread makers. **Examples** for white breads using all three yeasts on the shortest process achievable, avoiding residues and using your chosen yeast as a percentage of the flour weight: **Dried** 1.5%; **Fresh** 2.5%. **Mother** is a very basic yeast so will definitely expire when exposed to the intense heat of the bake. It also has many benefits, so can be added at much higher percentages, about 50% for the shortest term ferment. Rye breads will be added at much higher percentages, as explained later. The longest process we will work with will be overnight ferments.

This is calculated in the same way as a percentage of your flour weight. **Dried** 0.25%, reduced slightly from the 3/4 calculation, as it has to be released in the flying sponge to activate it. This will increase the available yeast spores, so slightly less is required. **Fresh** just 0.5% of the flour weight, and for the **Mother** 20% of the flour weight. This helps you understand just how basic these yeasts are by the volume necessary to achieve the same results in the same given time span.

WARNING

I have noticed that when I cover this primitive type of fermentation with cling film it retards (slows its activity down), so it is something I advise people to shy away from. These basic spores have more than enough to cope with, so don't put them through it. I understand there are now cling films made without the chemicals added, but I must admit I am reluctant to try them. It is such an unfriendly material to work with. Just use a plastic bag; this can be used time and time again and they are easy to slip over the bowl when you are all messy.

SALT IS AN IMPORTANT INGREDIENT

The importance of salt being added to bread is clearly underestimated, if you read the casual way it is used in so many bread recipes today. There is little point in lobbing in a couple of teaspoons as suggested by many. Salt is in there for many reasons, and particular attention should be paid to it when weighing out. It is hygroscopic so will complement the keeping quality of the crumb structure. It is in there for flavour, but most important, it is added to control the speed that the yeast will multiply at, so it quickly becomes one of the major ingredients added when controlling fermentation.

When setting the flying sponges, we put just flour, yeast and water together, and within forty minutes this had produced a cell, the yeast had quickly eaten all the available food within the vicinity of this cell, then naturally closed itself down to find fresh foods (this could help you understand optimum fermentation in the most primitive form). With no controls implemented whatsoever, job done in forty minutes.

If you put a small piece of fresh yeast onto the work surface and quickly work a small amount of salt into it then just watch as the salt kills the yeast, you will see it quickly start to go runny. When it is completely liquefied those yeast spores will have been killed, rendering them useless. It's worth remembering this when you come to weigh down a dough. If you are adding the yeast directly into all the ingredients, keep the yeast and the salt apart by weighing the salt to one side and the yeast to the other. If you put one on top of the other then go away to answer the phone and chat as long as my wife, on your return you will find they have liquefied. Naturally if you are unaware of this important fact, many of you will continue to make the dough but unfortunately you will be wasting your time. Nothing will happen; the dough will just sit there lifeless, or at the very least only have a small amount of the activity it should have. Your balanced dough has become out of balance at this very early stage of its life.

So look on yeast as being your accelerator: the more you add (within reason) the quicker the dough will ferment.

Look on salt as being the brake: this will control the speed that the yeast can multiply at. Put these two together in the dough and they will continually be fighting against each other, creating a natural balanced control.

Just as the salt is the brake, yeast will be the accelerator; then later the explanation of the dough temperature shows how that will become the fine tuning, making these the three most important factors in controlling this art. After calculating and weighing all of them accurately, everything after this will become add-ons to complement the process.

SALT ADDITION

Unfortunately bread has always been very political, right from the days when they would transport bakers to Australia for selling underweight bread, through the days of controlled weights, when the Weights and Measures man could legally stop you on the road or enter your shop to calculate the average weight of ten of your loaves, then kindly take you to court or give you a bad press if they were a few ounces underweight. We then had the bread subsidy enforced, generating reams of paperwork for the poor baker so that the misinformed government could keep the average price of the shopping basket down, doing damage to a basic food in doing so. The latest beating stick is the salt level in bread. Personally I would agree with the theory for many processed foods, as it has been used to excess in our quest for what would be bland convenience foods without it, but with bread it makes me nervous. It has taken so long for bread-making to gather momentum and for people to appreciate the flavours and the enjoyment it can bring to the table. Through being invited into bakeries to help them re-balance their recipes created by this low-salt request from the large retailers, I have noticed breads with reduced salt have become bland as well as uninteresting despite the addition of fermentation. There are many other ingredients I can think of within the modern breads that I would prefer to see taken out, or at least reduced; these never get a mention. It would be difficult for the volumes of bread we eat to be made without them if the supermarkets are to retain their horrendous profit margins. Maybe one day things will change.

There are also rumours of development going on with salt replacements. This can only be engineered, but why? There is a natural alternative, ground seaweed. This not only has a concentrated flavour, backing up the reduced salt levels, it is also a natural emulsifier, as well as a natural mould inhibiter, a fact I discovered accidently when trialling some years ago the natural raw sea salt crystals produced in the south of France. I'm not sure this will move forward in white breads, as it is inclined to discolour the final crumb colour we have grown accustomed to, but why not in wholemeal?

As always the rebel, I will be encouraging you to work with the standard percentage of salt, as this calculation has been used for many years throughout the industry. I wouldn't want to be responsible for harming anyone, so if you have a problem with salt, reduce it as you wish but you **must** remember its importance in controlling the process. If you reduce the salt, you must reduce the yeast as well to keep the dough in balance. They work hand in hand.

The other option is to be aware of the salt levels in foods you eat **with or on** the breads. Some of these, even after the reductions have been enforced, can be much higher than bread on its own. However, it is now a personal choice. At least making your own breads at home, it will be **you** making the decision rather than it being enforced on you by this strange culture that has evolved. Many things in our foods that are harmful to us are ignored for convenience and profit, other more simple ones that are easier to enforce become magnified to create a forced sense of wellbeing and to build trust in the decision makers.

NOTE

To satisfy my curiosity I ran trials under controlled conditions using specialised equipment in the test lab to see how much longer or shorter time a dough would need to reach optimum fermentation when altering the salt levels. Surprisingly, by increasing the salt by just 2g to 500g of white flour on an overnight ferment, instead of the normal fourteen hours allocated using 0.5% of fresh yeast, it took another two hours fifteen minutes before it started to fall back. At the same time I ran a comparison with 2g salt reduction; this peaked at eleven hours. Both trials were conducted in a controlled ambient temperature of 16°C.

I have trialled most of the salts. Table salt does the job but there are concerns for me with the anti-caking ingredients they use to prevent it becoming a brick. Salt is naturally hygroscopic so will always take on moisture from the atmosphere, making it difficult to flow without the anti-caking agents added. My Nan would always have a block of salt in her kitchen; to me as a young boy it seemed enormous and I was continually in trouble for boring holes in it with a knife. It didn't seem to worry her; she had to beat this to a powder to use it.

I favour the sea salts, although look closely; even some of these have the anti-caking ingredient added. If in doubt, go for the salt crystals, especially the raw sea salts with the traces of seaweed still in it, lovely to work with. I have found the dried ground seaweed in the health food shops; adding this to your product at 1.5% of the flour weight will mean you can reduce your salt addition by 30% and still have the same control and flavour. Once again, at home you can make what you want and live with the slight crumb decolouring. When the low salts first hit the market, I was encouraged by the manufacturers to conduct trials, with big disasters as a consequence. As with all things in bread, there will be an answer when using this product, and I have revisited this a few times, but it never seemed to be a top priority as there are so many other alternatives readily available as a much cheaper option.

WATER

As mentioned before, just simple tap water for me. It is pure enough not to influence the process, and also a luxury compared to the water I saw being hauled out of a well in the centre of the bakery when working in Tunisia while on holiday in 1986. It had this strange scum floating on the top of every bucket wound up. They assured me it was influenced by the sand but on peering down the hole, I became slightly suspicious of this explanation. But the breads made with it were a pleasure to eat, made by people who obviously knew their trade and how to work with the poor quality ingredients they had, and in extremely hot conditions too. Water when added to a dough (hydration) will vary from flour to flour. It will also vary from loaf to loaf, depending on your method or type of breads you want to make, so I would strongly advise you to use it as carefully as any other ingredient.

When added, always calculate it as a percentage of your flour and always weigh it on the scales. For ease of this calculation, look on it as a litre of water being a kilo of water. If you are using a jug and relying on the markings on the side, be aware that these alone can vary tremendously from jug to jug. Couple this with the fact you may well have the jug on a tilt when trying to look at these markings; your measurement could be a little too vague. Weigh the water into a jug on the scales; this precision will make it easy for you to make the small changes necessary if needed on the next production run. One thing you want to avoid is having to make adjustments to the dough through the development stage. If the dough is too tight, it is difficult to work extra water in. If the dough is too slack and you add more flour to help make it more manageable, in extreme cases you will be changing the ratio of the ingredients and unbalancing the dough.

Water can be replaced with milk or whey, even a proportion of buttermilk for the added texture. This will be used as a natural crumb and crust softener, as with our milk breads, but it would still need to be tempered (brought to the right temperature) before adding to ensure the dough is set so that it performs in the window allocated.

HYDRATION

If you analyse flour closely you will see it is made up of very small particles. Each one of these particles has a surface area all the way around it. The extent of this surface area is predetermined by the specification and the skill of the miller. When moisture is introduced to these particles, it clings to the outside wall of each of them. This encourages them to swell up, exposing the glutens (rubbery elastic parts) to hold the gas, also releasing the starches and natural maltose sugars to feed the yeast.

This hydration continues to take place as you proceed to develop (stretching and tearing) the dough, so naturally if anything has coated these particles before hydration has taken place, the moistures will be prevented from entering. This not only isolates the glutens that are needed to form a cell through the fermentation but also there will be nowhere for the allocated moistures to go, making your doughs feel incredibly sticky, tacky and unmanageable. **A lot of recipe books seem unaware** that adding oils or fats to a dough prematurely will do just that. This is one of the most important facts needed to determine the bite (crispy, soft, tough) of the finished article, so analyse your chosen recipe carefully and question the addition of these ingredients and when they are to be added. The products I have chosen to make with you through the basic range are designed to emphasise this **very important** fact. We will be using just one white flour for all products from breads right through the spectrum to short crust pastry; they all have their different qualities, all predetermined by when we add the ingredients and how much of them we add.

DEVELOPMENT OF THE GLUTEN

Development takes place while hydration is going on and this is the only time you can get aggressive with the dough. After this stage as it starts to ferment, forming a cell structure that is filling with gas, you will need to treat it with respect, folding and stretching rather than tearing. Doing this will encourage the yeast spores to reproduce and be retained within each new cell. If you are developing by hand this would be the ideal time to get anything that concerns you off your mind and go for it. It will make you a better person and also save you money by not having to go to the gym.

As with all steps of the bread making process, there are three stages, under, just right and over; development isn't any different. If mixing by hand, place all the dry ingredients into a large bowl, add the moisture and rub around until it starts to come together. Once past this stage, tip it out onto the work bench to start the development process. Everyone will find their own way of achieving this. I have seen many techniques applied around the table; they all work. Some take a little longer than others but the important point is to recognise optimum development rather than how you get there.

I personally, having done it so many times, have found the most efficient way to use my energy is use the heel of one hand, pulling it away from me in long determined strokes just above the work surface while holding the base with the other hand, slowly working my way down, covering more ground efficiently. The dough will pass through stages from being rough and rugged through lumpy and uneven (full of nuts and bolts to the touch) then becoming silky right through to ultra-smooth. This can be exhausting for some, so don't make a chore of it, as this may deter you from wanting to make your own breads. That is not the object of the exercise. Mix it for a few minutes, then rest it and yourself for a minute, then mix for a few minutes, then rest for a few minutes, until that ultra-silky feel starts to appear.

This logic still needs to be applied when working with some of the small overpriced domestic mixers, KitchenAid or Kenwood for example, just to respect the small under-powered motor they put into them for bread making. This will help them to last longer. When using these mixers there can be a danger of over-developing if you mix too aggressively for too long. You will recognise this when it turns from a silky smooth clean feel to a sticky and tacky mess that wants to become attached to you when you touch it. So once again touch and feel will be the skill you acquire to help you along the way.

Even if you have a mixer to help, it may be as well to develop your first few attempts by hand to gain this understanding. This over-development happens because the strands you have been encouraging to take the moistures on board as you develop them will start to become over-starched, causing them to snap, thus releasing the moistures they have retained. It won't be irretrievable if recognised early; just let it rest for a little while before gently folding a few times to encourage them back into their right place. Never be tempted to add more flour to the dough; if you have it perfectly balanced this will change the ratio. This fault can be detrimental to the final crumb structure if practised to the extreme, making it fragile and dry within a very short time after baking. I have only seen this occur a few times when hand development is practiced around the bench. If this does happen, I will be very mindful how I offer my guidance, offering it to the maker from the other end of the room close to the door.

TEMPERATURE CONTROL

This is the final most important influence on setting the dough. The dough activity (the speed it ferments at) is controlled not only by the amount of yeast and salt added in the dough but also influenced greatly by temperature. This will fine-tune everything. When you are just starting out it is best to aim for the average figure that fermentation is most comfortable with. Yes, there will be exceptions to this rule but best not to get involved with these in the early stages. You need to set your doughs at the magic figure of 25°C to 28°C. Too low and the dough will take longer to get started, too high and there will be a danger of it over-fermenting in the time allocated, because the cells will start multiplying and become out of control too soon. The importance of this fact applies only to the first hour or so of its life in the dough state. This will ensure the chain reaction has started; then it can carry on even if the ambient temperature (in the kitchen) is lower. Yes, you could get clinical and maintain the dough at 16°C to 18°C after the first hour but this isn't one of the most important factors. I wouldn't want to encourage you to put it on the radiator or in the airing cupboard; an even ambient temperature will be better, as continually changing it will cause confusion and affect the finished article.

How do we achieve this? This is where your temperature gauge or thermometer comes in useful. The two main ingredients in a loaf of bread are the flour and water. The flour will fluctuate in temperature on a weekly basis or if you have just received a fresh delivery. If we lived in an ideal world and the flour was always running at, say, 28°C and you then add water to the dough at 28°C, then when these two ingredients are blended together they will naturally be roughly 28°C. The ideal world, however, will never be; flour temperature will always change.

Take your chosen finished dough temperature and multiply that by two, say, 28°C x 2 = 56°C, then take your probe and push it into the flour for a temperature reading.

Whatever this reads, you will need to take this figure away from the 56°C calculated by doubling your chosen controlling factor.

Summer Example: say your flour in the summer is running at 18°C. Take eighteen from fifty-six; this equals 38°C. You would then need to blend hot and cold water together until it reaches this temperature.

Winter Example: your flour could be as low as 10°C; fifty-six will still be the controlling figure minus the ten degrees of the flour. The water then would need to be blended to reach 46°C. Doing it this way eliminates the necessity to keep your flour somewhere warm or heating the flour in the oven before you start and some of the many other unnecessary complications I have seen.

Even after these calculations have been implemented, there may be other factors to take into account. If you enjoy precision it may be worth your noting, as I have, having worked with so many people around the bench, that you see a variety of different personalities coming through when people are developing their doughs by hand. Although we all start out with flour and water at the same temperature, having calculated to keep it between the magic 25°C to 28°C, some people with a gentle personality will struggle to creep in, just getting to the bottom of these boundaries, while others with outward-going energy will attack it with aggression, increasing the temperature over and above the boundaries (these I send on anger management courses). This is why bread can reflect your personality. When I feel good inside, it looks better; when I feel bad inside, it won't be so good. Trust me, this is fact.

If you are working with a planetary mixer, even these small ones at home can put in up to 7°C worth of energy, so you may need to adjust the water temperature in accordance with this fact. Some of the industrial mixers I have worked on in bakeries can add up to 20°C worth of energy. This makes it very difficult to work with through the summer months, so crushed ice is added to balance it all out. If you are developing on a wood surface by hand, little heat will be lost, but if you are developing on a granite or marble surface by hand through the winter months, many degrees can be sucked out through the process. So once again make the adjustment to compensate for this. This is now your skill. Continually use your probe all through the process to complement this skill and make the right decisions to control the process, helping you to be in control, not the elements.

Historically in small bakeries they would mix a very large amount of dough by hand in dough troughs. These were traditionally made from maple wood as this wood is less likely to splinter. It also has the added advantage of eventually becoming hard and impervious with continual use, if treated right. They would place all the dry ingredients into the trough, add the water, then travel down through the trough, using the whole of the length of both arms and hands with a crossover motion to bring them together in a motion emulated on the very first Artofex mechanical mixer. They would then rest it for ten or fifteen minutes, then start to cut back, using a very large bull-nose knife, as a pointed one could have been in danger of digging into the wood. Slowly and methodically they would work their way down, scooping up large amounts of dough over one arm and stretching upward before cutting back with the knife with the other hand until reaching the other end. A further rest was given each time, followed by repeating the cut backs with the bull nose knife. I have done it a few times in the past when we experienced many power cuts through the blackout strike years in the seventies; the dough comes together surprisingly quickly, but we were very grateful of the rest when the power came back on and my primitive but effective signal-arm Dumbril mixer could earn its keep again. Some nights this mixer would be set to its full capacity of 350 lb of flour in those days, 150 kg or so in today's weight, plus the water making over 250 kg of dough in total, including the other ingredients. Once mixed, this would be transferred to the wooden dough troughs to slow ferment through the night.

Sadly this practice had to stop when Health and Safety visited one day to inform me that wood was a health risk in the bakery environment. It would now have to be replaced with unfriendly clinical cold stainless steel or some manufactured plastic that, as it happens, would scar deeply when knives and scrapers were used on it, harbouring germs that can multiply unless bleached. Fermentation and sterilisation don't go well together. Unfortunately plastic wouldn't have the ability to heal itself as wood will if treated right. My then newly-invested-in pride and joy, acquired at great expense with time and money I could ill afford to waste, then became a rather large ornamental flower tub in the yard. Over the next thirty years this opinion has changed as they've educated themselves to learn that wood has natural inhibiters within it, so once again it is acceptable to use. This can be proven if you put Mother into an unseasoned wooden vessel or bare wooden cupboard; she will become sluggish and eventually die, a problem experienced by one or two bakers who live in green-oak-framed buildings.

Once the dough had been set into the troughs and it had had its allocated bulk fermentation time, it would then receive a knock-back in its entirety, if mixed by hand, to strengthen it. The baker would then replace the wooden lids, placing a couple of rolling pins on the top, so he could go and have an hour or so's extra sleep on the flour bags. He curled up next to the cat, in full confidence that as the dough proved up, it would push the lids up. They would inevitably tilt, tipping the rolling pins off onto the floor and making a noise to wake them both up. It didn't work for me when I put it into practice, as I had become exhausted trying to keep production going in extremely difficult circumstances of three days with power and two days without for many months. I did learn, however, how to salvage something that had gone way over its bulk time allocated; everything has a reason and we all learn from our mistakes.

FATS AND OILS

All fats and oils have a big impact on the final product, so careful thought should be given to when you are adding them, as suggested earlier. If they are being added at low percentages as an extender (to complement the elasticity within the functional glutens) they must be added after hydration has taken place, or about half way through the development stage is a good guide. Just add them and continue mixing; they will soon disappear. This will ensure they have no influence in coating the small particles of flour, creating the problem of isolating them from the moistures. This will become even more important when we come to making the enriched products such as the sweet bun dough later. We will be expecting this dough to carry from 15% to 20% of the flour weight in butter. In extreme cases such as the Brioche it will be as high as 50% of the flour weight, hence the necessity to develop the dough first, add half the butter, then refrigerate before adding the remainder. If you read a recipe for a bread or bun made with the fats added to the flour before the moisture, it will give you a problem. Don't put yourself through it.

Later on when we come to making the short crust pastry or scones to demonstrate this fact, we will be working right to the other end of the spectrum, utilising our fats to isolate the functional glutens within the flour before the liquids are added, preventing hydration from taking place. This will determine the shortness we require.

Through the bad days in our baking history, our simple enriched products such as the Bath bun, Chelsea bun, lardy cake and so on seemed to fall by the wayside, with the reputation of being unhealthy for their sugar and fat content. Our bun goods traditionally have only 15% fats; strangely, these became replaced with products such as the Brioche, 50% fat, and Danish pastry, 40% fat. Over the past few years it has been good to see a bit of a revival going on with our own products. Keep it up; fly the flag. What happened to the dough cake, where did that go? I'll give you a recipe for that one later; it's good for using up old dough if you over-produce.

There are four pure fats or oils traditionally used in baking. I favour these for taste, quality and the functional properties they will bring to the end results. They are lard, butter, olive oil or palm fats for the organic option. I dismiss all the other engineered products; I have seen them being made, and ask, Why? Historically lard would have been the only affordable fat used in this country. It would be added in small amounts to our breads to enhance the keeping quality and bring an added flavour of its own to the finished article. For this purpose I would normally run (add) no higher than 2% of my flour weight on a white flour and perhaps 3% on some wholemeal, especially stone ground flour to help coat the bran.

SOYA

Soya flour is readily available in most health food shops; I use it in fermented products in small proportions, no more than 2% of the flour weight. It works as a natural emulsifier through the process to help soften the crumb; it will also absorb twice its own weight in water, helping the product to retain more moisture for longer, so helping it to stay fresher. You will need keep this in mind when you choose to use it in recipes that it is not stipulated in. When experimenting, increase the hydration by twice as much as the weight of soya flour added to the recipe.

MALT EXTRACT

Once again, this is readily available through health food shops and some chemists, mainly in a liquid form in a jar. It can be a little difficult to handle; using a hot wet teaspoon will help. There will also be a product on the shelf marked cod-liver oil and malt extract; this is not so nice when added to bread, so be vigilant when making your purchase. I have accumulated a few of these in the past. As children we were brought up on a combination of cod-liver oil and sticky malt extract; sadly the cod-liver oil was served up as neat liquid on a spoon followed very quickly by the malt extract to get rid of the taste. On reflection, not all things from the past were the best. Strangely, the jar of malt extract seemed to go down more quickly than the cod-liver oil, something Mum could never really understand.

Malt products are very useful for helping crust retention on longer ferments. The natural sugars within them are the same as the natural maltose sugars within the flour. It will also bring a subtle natural sweetness to products such as baps and dinner rolls, rather than using purified sugar. In the industry there is a wide range of these dried malts available. These can be added to flours at high proportions with malted flakes to create the branded malted breads such as Granary, incidentally nothing like the original product when first marketed by two young lads who developed it. The changes took place when a larger mill bought the marketing rights to it and a name became more marketable than the quality. The dried malt flour and flakes are available through some millers, and I have seen the flakes in the health food shops but not the malt flours yet. For the more advanced, there are active and non-active malt products; the active ones should be used very sparingly within breads, so are not recommended as this can create more problems than they will solve if not applied to the right product. These are mainly used for the dense sticky malt breads and I have never seen them on the domestic market; they are only obtainable, as far as I know, through the specialist manufacturers. In standard breads the malt extracts are added at 1% to 1.5% of the flour weight and I have found little advantage to increasing above this amount.

Overnight Ferments (sponges)

This is the first dough we will make together, using the most basic of recipes with the shortest time allocated, while encouraging you to dip your toe into fermentation.

You only have to go back two generations to find all our bakers making all of their breads on the long slow overnight fermentation process. They knew nothing different. To do this, the last thing they would do before they went home was to set their doughs for the next day's production. This would mean that the bakers could come straight in after the time allocated to start working with it, giving them slightly longer to rest between shifts. Slowly as the demand for breads made by the baker grew rather than their being made at home, the baker found it more difficult to have these large amounts of dough lying around overnight, hence the birth of the sponge and dough. The overnight dough would still be made up and the premium overnight breads would be taken off it in the morning for the people who still demanded this bread. They were prepared to pay a higher price for it (half a penny in my day). The remainder of the overnight dough would then be added at various set amounts to the other range of breads, using it as a concentrated ferment to enhance and complement a short term dough.

The shortest ferment that you can lend to any process will be about two and a quarter hours in total, excluding the bake: 1 hour's bulk proof, 20 minutes' intermediate proof, 20 to 50 minutes' final proof, dependent on the product. This will be rather bland in flavour, with a soft crust with a tendency to be temperamental, even with the controls implemented. If you add something natural, such as a set proportion of well-fermented dough, you will be adding time to it. This will be in the form of concentrated acidity within this portion of the added dough. This then will start to work within the whole of the dough, emulating all the assets of a six-hour controlled fermentation with reference to taste, crumb and crust. It is also better for the digestion. This practice is well worth doing at home in the domestic kitchen, but it can be a bit of a pain to remember to set such a small amount of dough the night before and it will inevitably get forgotten, so working with a pinch back sitting in your fridge will make sure it is always ready and waiting for you. The first time you venture out on this method you won't have any sponge ready, so you will need to set down (mix and leave overnight) just the once for the first one, enough of your chosen volume of flour to start. The minimum amount of sponge you can add to see its full benefits will be about 25% to 30% of your flour weight within the main recipe. Many bakers now, thankfully, do work with higher percentages to make their products different, but for educational purposes we will limit it to an average of 30% of the flour weight in your recipe to make sure you have enough.

Once you have made the sponge and it has had its minimum time of at least 14 hours at the ambient temperature, you can choose to pop it in the fridge until you are ready to make your breads. It can sit in there for up to a week, provided you have covered it to prevent it skinning. Yes, it will go slack and tacky as the yeast depletes but we won't be using it for the yeasts. We will be using it in our main dough as a concentrated acidity, to enhance all the necessary attributes within the main dough we add it to. When you are ready to make your dough, this will be brought out and added as a percentage of your flour weight, just as any other ingredient, but remember it will be cold, so it is advisable to work to the top end of your temperature calculations to compensate for this fact. And then there may be other small adjustments to make on the next run if you find you are a little low.

You may decide to make your breads straight away, so the sponge will be at a more realistic ambient temperature, making it necessary to work at the bottom end of the temperature calculations to maintain balance. This is a skill that will become second nature to you with practice. If you make bread on a daily basis, then just make up one sponge, enough to cover your week's production, and keep it in the fridge, ready to pinch off the required amount for each day's production. When you have practiced working with percentages, you will quickly be able to work out a recipe for the overnight sponge, making it large enough to make, say, one large loaf and process it as a traditional white bread, then keeping enough back to make a sponge and dough method in the two and a half hours window necessary for it.

When you are starting to get confidence in your skills, try the overnight ferment, giving it the full 14 hours necessary, then just knock it back (push the gas out by stretching the cells rather than tearing) and place it in the fridge, covered, for a further 6 to 8 hours before processing. This will really sing on the palate. I add this all in not to confuse but to show you how you can adapt any process to work to your advantage once you have mastered control when setting down your chosen dough. All these add-ons may be difficult to control if the basics have not been implemented at the start. When you come to eat all of these different breads made from the same recipe, with the only ingredient being changed being the time allocated, you will soon appreciate the importance of this ingredient and the benefits it can bring, not only to the palate but after time you will realise its benefits to your digestion as well.

If you choose to use the pinch back method, you will need to set the sponge for the first production the night before. When it has had its time, you will incorporate this into the main dough about half way through the development stage. This needs to be done at this stage as the strands in this small part of the dough have not only been fully developed to their full extent from a mechanical point (mixing) but also from a fermentation point as well, giving it a tendency to be fragile if added too soon into the main part of the dough. This will cause the strands to fracture and release their moistures while you are trying to develop the new strands in the main dough. Once this dough has had its full time allocated for the bulk proof, you can pinch off your required weight for your next production, pop it into the fridge covered ready for the next run, then you are away; just keep rolling it over.

Skilly wash

This is used for many reasons and is such a simple add-on to your baking skills. It will keep the dough supple for longer when the heat hits the surface, preventing it from setting too early, which causes it to pinch back and burst randomly in unexpected places. As the heat hits the surface of the loaf washed with it, this will help to gelatinise all those surface starches you have worked so hard to create, especially if complemented with adding steam into the chamber (oven) in some way or another. When the surface starches are scalded, it will enhance the bloom (shine to the crust) on the surface. If you wash the loaf with water before sticking seeds on to decorate, they will always fall off as soon as you touch them after baking, ending up over the floor or at the very best on the bread board. If you wash with egg or milk, both of which are protein, the protein will soften the crust retention. Save these for the enriched products or morning rolls when you need to create a softer crust.

Using scalded starches will help complement the finished article on crusty products. Corn flour being the purest of starches is the one I favour. When making this, keep in mind the making of a custard. It is the same principle, but using pure corn flour instead of custard powder and water instead of milk. Nothing like custard then! But the method will be applicable. Place a couple of large teaspoons of corn flour into a vessel large enough to carry about a quarter of a litre of liquid. Add just enough cold water to this to form a thin paste. Boil the kettle, keeping your finger on the button to ensure you have passed boiling point, then carefully pour the water over the corn flour blend, whisking with a fork as you do so until it resembles a thin clear paste. If it doesn't reach this condition on the first attempt then you can pop it into the microwave for a minute, if you have one, to add the extra heat needed to coagulate the starch. Once cooled this can be applied to your breads for its obvious benefits or can be kept in the refrigerator for a week before it starts to break down.

Here we go then: Basic Workshop

When making this recipe in the workshop with a few of us around the table, I have identified the products we make from this dough to help to demonstrate the importance of each stage of this part of the process. Obviously you can make it into the shape you want, but read through the descriptions of each part of the process to help you to implement some of the techniques needed to achieve good results.

The Cottage loaf historically is a big part of our baking heritage and has been with us for many hundreds of years, until it became a problem to fit in with the uniform shape of a sandwich. In fact the terminology 'upper crust' when referring to the lucky people who got to sit on the top table at banquets refers to this bread. Bread then would have been made from really basic primitive grain, roughly ground, possibly without any form of basic fermentation lent to it. It would be made into a rough dough and baked in a wood-fired oven, resulting in it being very hard and crusty to eat. The elite would then demand something special (as they do) and this was to be the answer: put one piece of dough on the top of the other and when baked this would be of a lighter bake with a soft underbelly, without the added roughage of ash or lumps of charred wood, as this part had no contact with the sole (floor) of the oven. The remnants would be thrown down to the peasants such as myself sitting at the lower tables, for them to soften it down in their gruel or stew, and probably be very gratefully received by us in those days. Making this loaf will give you more chances to practice your moulding techniques, ensuring you create tension through the internal cell structure without tearing the outer surface. You will also be balancing one piece of dough on top of the other, so if your dough is unhappy this process will magnify it. It will be a free-standing loaf set on the sole or hot tray in the oven. If it is not happy, this will once again magnify any imbalance by falling back as the heat penetrates, resulting in the head falling back into the shoulders of the loaf if the cell structure starts to fracture prematurely.

Three-strand plait will be practised for two reasons; one, to give a little bit of an insight into some of the fancy breads traditionally produced, a three-strand being one of the simplest. To learn this art as a young apprentice, I was sent to work with the very skilled Jewish bakers in London. What an education! I have great respect for the people I worked with. For competition work they would plait with up to twenty-eight strands. I personally never reached this level of skill but did eventually complete my way through to eighteen without dropping a stitch (not sure I could remember now). This skill is soon forgotten if not practised. The second reason is to magnify the importance of moulding. When moulding, the art is to confuse the cell structure by stretching the extending cells over each other, not only to reintroduce them to fresh foods but to also ensure they cross over each other, creating a finer even crumb structure. If you have difficulty in moulding, then plaiting can help to overcome this, even if your choice of product is the tin loaf. This is the reason the original Jewish Challahs were produced on a four-strand plait; it was an enriched dough but also expected to have an exceptionally fine crumb.

Pitta I slip in here to help demonstrate gas retention within a cell; it was also a fantastic bread to eat when made by individuals. Sadly this is no longer the case now as it represents the sole of a shoe with little hope of it opening for good presentation. This changed when it was forced into a price war by the powers that be, with streamlining and mass production taking over. It was a revelation for me through the eighties to be able to go and work with the many Greek bakers who had by then settled in London, hoping to gain their trust and in doing so sell them flour. It was such a simple way to utilise bread to feed yourself when produced in extreme ambient temperatures in their own country. Originally it would be set using a Mother dough but will work very well with a yeast on any flour, including wholemeal, providing it is reasonably finely ground. The very thing they have dispensed with in this simple bread when being mass produced was once again fermentation.

Here we go again, sorry; I have so many snippets of information to pass on to you to help you understand the world you are entering. Through the mid to late nineties on visiting what had become one of the largest producers of these types of bread then, I was just hoping to gain some support from them for the small independent miller, and in doing so be able to take small amounts of flour trade from the very aggressive larger corporate miller. They definitely frowned on the independent miller trying to gain a foothold in what had almost become a cartel, so much so that on many occasions I would question my parentage after bumping into their representatives, having previously taken trade from them somewhere.

One day the big man at the top of the tree in this bakery, who rarely saw the likes of me, invited me in to put into practice the customer support that I had promised so many times to their buyer and middle management each time I visited. They had been instructed by one of their large customers to produce a range of organic pittas. The problem they had was the shelf life of the finished article. This would be very limited as it was having to be produced on such a short bake to keep it supple, and this would leave a lot of moisture in the final bake. Moisture will encourage mould spores if nothing is applied to control it. Although, sadly, organic improvers had been approved by this time, sensibly the controlling bodies would not permit the use of the common ingredient added to control the moulds on conventional breads, called calcium propionate, suggesting they substitute it with organic white wine vinegar. True, it slows the growth down, but in something so small and barely baked that it does not evaporate the spirit, it certainly left an undesirable after-taste. The acidity in the vinegar was logical, as there are lots of concentrated acidities within the Mother dough. Traditional rye breads produced in Germany and many parts of Europe are not eaten until they have been matured for ten days, and they never show signs of mould spores if kept in the right conditions. So rye Mother was applied to the dough with this logic. After many trials conducted over many weeks to find the optimum level, success was achieved.

This was to win the trade for a short while for the company I worked for, but the knowledge applied was soon to be forgotten when incentives were offered by the opposition to gain the trade back. This wasn't a reflection on the bakery; you could hardly blame them, as the people employed to balance the books for the company came under constant price pressure from the larger retailer, with their schemes to continually drive their prices down to maintain their own large profit margins.

EXAMPLE

We are really starting work now

RECIPE FOR SPONGE IF YOU ARE STARTING FROM SCRATCH

INGREDIENTS	%		GRAMS
White flour	100		100
Salt	2	1 x 2 = 2	2
Yeast (Fresh)*	1	1 x 1 = 1	1
Water	60	60 x 1 = 60	60
		Total	160

*If using the active dried yeast then you will still have to run with the 1g, as most domestic scales will not weigh below this. It won't be so critical in this part of the dough as it will be added to the main dough later. All we want to do is create concentrated acidity. It will also need to be activated first. To do this, take roughly half the flour, all the water, all the yeast, beaten together; this will only need to sit for ten minutes, just until the beads have dispersed, rather than the full forty minutes needed for the flying sponge. Then add to the remaining flour and process (mix).

Finished dough temperature 25°C to 28°C; using the calculation of twice the finished dough temperature chosen, in this case it should be 28°C, minus the flour temperature you have at the time. The remaining figure will determine the water temperature needed to balance everything. Once again, this is not so critical on this small dough but well worth getting the practice in.

METHOD

Weigh the flour into a bowl, then weigh the salt on the top, making sure it is put to one side; weigh the yeast, placing it on the opposite side just as a precaution. Pour in the allocated water that has been previously weighed; don't try to weigh it directly on the top of the flour as it is difficult to take it out if you are being over-generous.

DEVELOPMENT

Bring this to rough dough; it will be small in size so better to just use your finger tips to start. You are now encouraging the moistures to hydrate into the flour. This will be done by continually fluffing it through, rather than stretching and tearing, until there aren't any flour particles exposed. It will now be of a rough uneven texture. Tip it out onto the work surface to start the development. As explained earlier, you will develop your own technique. It doesn't matter how you get there as long as you get there. Having mixed so many of them by hand, I have learnt to use my energy efficiently, so I will attempt to describe the actions to help you along the way.

Tip out onto the work surface, then using the heel of one hand, start sliding in long positive strokes away from you from the bottom upwards, keeping the heel of the hand just above the work surface. This will create a grinding affect against the surface as you go. Repeat, choosing a different area to cover each time you return from the bottom to the top. Every now and then, scrape up all the rough bits from the edges to the centre, which also frees it from the work surface. This will need to be repeated until it has all come together. Once it starts to form a rough-textured dough, the elasticity will start to kick in. You will then need to start holding the bottom end of the dough with the other hand while working your way down, stretching and tearing. This will prevent it from keeping on springing back, wasting your energy on each stroke. Slowly it will start to become smoother and smoother with every stroke as you continue with the process.

This is a small dough so won't take much effort to complete, but when you start on the larger main dough you may need to take a couple of rests as you progress, just for a minute or so. This will make the job easier for you; rest and mix, rest and mix, and as you do this you will see how quickly you and the dough recover, creating a smoother, silkier, soft, almost skin-like feel to the finished dough. If you are happy, then keep right on with it all the way through. There are many ways to achieve this; hopefully this will just help you to get into a rhythm while you are finding your own technique. Silky smooth is what you want and nothing less.

Once completed, put back into the bowl and cover, and place somewhere in the corner of the kitchen for 14 hours. It will still be all right if you can't get to it for 18 hours, but after this time you may well be pushing your luck, so if you can't process it for any time after the 14 hours, pop it into the fridge until you can. This can wait for a week or more once chilled down, but will deteriorate if it is left at an ambient room temperature, giving the finished loaf an unpleasant taste.

MAIN DOUGH			
INGREDIENTS	%		GRAMS
White flour	100		500
Salt	2	2 x 5 = 10	10
Fresh yeast	2	2 x 5 = 10	10
Sponge (pinch back)	30	30 x 5 = 150	150
Water	60	60 x 5 = 300	300
		Total	970
WHOLEMEAL			
Stoneground wholemeal	100		500
Salt	2	2 x 5 = 10	10
Yeast	2	2 x 5 = 10	10
Lard	2	2 x 5 = 10	10
White sponge	30	30 x 5 = 150	150
Water	70	70 x 5 = 350	350
		Total	1030

Finished dough temperature 25°C to 28°C using the tempered water with the right calculations 28 x 2 = 56 – flour temperature = water temperature.

METHOD

Weigh the flour, salt, and yeast into a large bowl, remembering to keep the two small ingredients apart. If making the wholemeal, don't add the fat yet.

Temper the water to the right degree and weigh into a separate vessel ready to use.

Make sure you have made the adjustments to the water temperature; if using the sponge from the fridge, work to top end of the temperature specification. If the sponge has been sitting at an ambient temperature, the bottom end of the specification, 25°C, is a good guide.

Have the correct weight of sponge and the lard close by, ready to add halfway through the development.

Add the water to the large bowl containing the flour, salt and yeast.

Continue to develop as we did before when setting the sponge. It will be a little harder work than the small dough if developing by hand, but stick with it until it becomes silky smooth to the touch.

When the dough has come together and is becoming partly stretchy, this will indicate that the moistures have hydrated well into the flour particles. You can then add the sponge to the white, and sponge and lard to the wholemeal, with confidence that the lard will do no harm and the sponge will not become overdeveloped towards the end of the process.

If using a mechanical mixer, still mix and rest to avoid over-loading, which could cause damage to the machine.

Once fully developed, scuff up (form a neat ball) and place back into the bowl, cover to avoid skinning, and put to one side in the corner of the kitchen for 1 hour (bulk proof). Because this dough has been set to a control, this bulk proof time won't need to be set in stone. You can leave it a little longer rather than shorter, but I wouldn't chance much more than 1½ hours when starting out.

MOULDING (SCUFFING UP, HANDING UP)

Moulding is a critical part of the process and well worth pratising when the dough is in the dead state (no gas), so when you have finished the development stage, this is a good time to have a practice. Once gas has formed, you only want to re-introduce the yeasts to fresh food, so if you practice moulding for too long after the gas has formed, there is a danger of over-moulding, causing you to enter the development stage again, rather than the stretching needed.

There are many different moulding techniques, and it took me five years of regularly being clipped around the ear before I mastered them using both hands, with one loaf in each hand. Every morning I was continually being reminded I was paid to use two hands, not one, and if I continued to use one hand the boss would only pay me half my salary. This did become an incentive to me, so don't get disheartened.

All you are really doing is taking the outside surface and folding it into the centre to ensure each cell is being stretched rather than torn. The round shape is the best one to demonstrate this. To scuff up, place the developed dough piece onto the work surface, ensuring it is not sticking. There is no need to use flour; the dough should be clean and free from you and the workbench. Press out, using the heel of your hand to form a circle, then start to pull out one part of the edge of the circle, stretching it over itself to the centre of the circle. This needs to be repeated all the way around the edge until you get back to where you started. When completed, turn the dough piece right over so that all the seams are underneath, revealing a smooth surface on the top.

You now need to apply pressure to the base of this, using the edge of both hands, trying to make the edges of each hand touch against each other, pulling one against the other, pushing one up while pulling the down with the other. This needs to be repeated until the outside surface starts to become smooth. When doing this action after the gas has formed, there is a danger the outside surface will start to tear. This is a good indication that you have pushed it as far as it wants to go and the cells are starting to fracture. If this happens in the dead state while you are practising, it's not a problem; it has plenty of time to recover. It will be more important when it has gas retention.

After the bulk proof, we start scaling into the units required, handing up followed by the very important intermediate proof, to produce the range of breads I suggested at the start. Producing this range will give you as many opportunities as possible to learn something different about processing a dough with the limited volume of dough we have to work with. We will scale into various sizes, but if you follow the same procedure, making any size or shape you want, it will work just as well.

In case you do move forward into producing larger amounts of bread to sell, you will need to be aware of the Weights and Measures Act. The weight of dough in the recipe above could produce just one large loaf, if you want, with a finished baked weight when cooled of 850g, just over the traditional minimum legal weight to conform with the legal requirements of 800g for a large, 400g for a small loaf. Anything under 250g would be classed as speciality breads, so did not have to conform to any weight controls. Things are changing slowly, to fall into line with the European legislation, and as long as it is wrapped and clearly marked with its finished weight, it will be outside their controls, but who wants to wrap bread? If you do, I would favour thick paper bags that can breathe rather than plastic, which would encourage the product to sweat, deteriorating the crust and encouraging mould growth.

PROCESSING THE DOUGH

When you bring forward the dough, having given it its full bulk proof time, covered with another plastic bowl or a plastic bag or even just a simple wooden bread board will suffice, as you take off the cover you will smell the lovely sweet aromas of the fermentation given off as this process has been taking place. Having it covered in this way will ensure that none of the moisture being expelled through this stage will have been lost. As these droplets will have precious spores within them, covering the dough will encourage them to fall back onto the surface of the dough. As you will feel to the touch when first exposed, one reason never to cover with a wet tea towel is that the dough's moisture will just get absorbed into the moist cover, being lost for ever. This is not one of the most important facts but a fact never the less.

Take note of the amount of gas retained and the amount of time it has taken to achieve this; it will help you appreciate the extra activity achieved through one simple knock-back later on through the process. This will be because the yeast cells are being encouraged to multiply, gathering speed as they do so. After 1 hour's bulk proof, knock back, and there will be as much activity within it after just 20 minutes' intermediate proof.

PINCH BACK

If you are choosing to work with the pinch back system, to eliminate the need to remember to make the sponge the night before, this would be the time to take it off. So, for instance, if you were going to make the same size dough next time, you would need to cut off 150g of the dough to place into the fridge in a container with a lid on to prevent skinning. This can sit in the fridge for a week or 10 days; yes, it will go slack and tacky naturally as the yeasts deplete, but we will not be adding it to the next dough for the yeasts. It will be added for the concentrated acidities and the benefits they will bring to the product.

If you do put this into practice, you will obviously be 150g short on the dough weight for the range we make below, so you can decide either to adjust the recipe by increasing the flour content by 100g followed by the right percentages of the other ingredients, or simply eliminate the production of the pitta. This adjustment would only need to be made once; from then on you will always have it sitting in the fridge ready. You have now created the pinch back or roll over system (you are in control, not the recipe book).

Tip out the dough without damaging too many of the cells formed. If you are concerned about it sticking, you may need to lightly dust the work surface to start, but as you get used to handling it, this shouldn't be necessary, especially if you are working on a wooden work surface. It is so user friendly. Once the bowl is empty, just turn it over to make a nice little moist environment to tuck the dough pieces under as you scale them off. This will prevent them from skinning up, helping to keep them supple when you come to mould them. To scale off the units, it would be better to chop with a scraper or cut with a knife rather than tear, as tearing will damage too many cells.

For the cottage loaf scale off a unit of 450g, about half the complete dough. Chop it through and place on the scales; if short, chop smaller pieces and add to bring it to the right weight. If too large, then chop off small pieces to reduce the weight. When the right weight has been achieved, tuck under the bowl in a rough shape while you proceed to weigh the others.

For the pittas weigh 2 pieces, if producing the white, or 3 for the wholemeal, at 50g and tuck under the bowl.

Three strand plait: the remainder will need to be divided into 3 equal-sized pieces, and in theory it should equate to 140g a piece, but this is rarely achieved in practice. There will always be small variations that won't warrant worrying about; they will all be going back together when we come to making the plait. What we need to achieve is a uniform shape; equal weights will help with the presentation of the finished article.

Once the 3 have been scaled, tuck under the bowl, at the same time bringing out the very first one you scaled off, the 450g piece, to start the moulding process.

OVENS AND BAKING

The products we are making from this dough will all require relatively short final proof because of the controls and attention we paid to them at the start, so you will now need to turn on your oven to make sure it is up to temperature when you need it. All ovens are different, and you will have learnt the best way to work with yours, I'm sure, but as a guide I would set this type of bread into a chamber running at 220°C to 230°C. I really only have two temperatures I work with on fermented goods, this being the savoury control. If it is sweetened or enriched, I drop to 200°C to 210°C.

We will be baking these breads on the sole (base) of the oven. Normally in industrial ovens this is of stone or a similar product that can retain heat. To ensure that the breads are set in the right environment to complete the final stages of the process, all breads, including tin breads, need to be placed directly onto a hot sole to ensure the base is set first, then the top surface needs to be kept as moist and supple as possible for as long as possible, to ensure it is encouraged to grow and expand evenly.

Most domestic ovens do not have a solid base, so to help emulate this, something that conducts heat readily, like a cast iron skillet or the thickest baking tray you have, will suffice. There is no need to go to the great expense of a pizza stone; some of them are a bit overpriced. Utilise what you have in the kitchen. This then needs to be placed into the chamber on the rack about a third of the way up in the chamber.

Later we will be adding steam to the chamber for a couple of reasons, one, to help keep the surface supple, and two, to scald the surface starches. This will help them gelatinise, creating a bloom and also complementing the crust retention, so when you turn the oven on you will need to place a shallow baking dish with sides at the bottom of the oven. This will ensure that it is as hot as it can be when you come to set the loaves into the chamber. When the loaves are set, half a cup of cold water is thrown directly into this pan and the door closed as quickly as possible, ensuring the steam created is trapped within the chamber to do its job. Once trapped, the steam travels to the top, then when it falls back down onto the surface of the loaf, it scalds all the surface starches created through the fermentation process, helping to enhance a crisper crust. It also helps to keep the external exposed surface supple for longer, preventing it from pinching back and creating a deformed final shape as the energy struggles to escape. For these breads, there is little point in adding a tin with water in when you turn the oven on, or throwing ice cubes into a hot pan. They will bounce around for ages, giving off small amounts of steam for long periods. You want the two extremes: hot pan, cold water, in whoosh, door shut, job done.

MOULDING OR HANDING UP READY FOR THE INTERMEDIATE PROOF

Through this part of the process, flour or oil should not need to be added to the work surface. If the dough has been balanced right from the start, you should be able to keep it free from both you and the work surface without them.

When you take it from under the bowl it will be rough in appearance and full of gas. Now is the time to give it the first mould, ready for the intermediate proof. This is done just as we practised when the dough was in the dead state but it will be more relaxed to start with.

Using your scraper, ensure the dough piece is free from the work surface. Press out lightly, using the palm of the hand, then starting from the outside, start pulling and stretching over to the centre. Repeat this action all the way around until you get back to where you started, then turn over so the seams are all on the base and the reasonably smooth surface is facing up.

Now continue with the pressing at the base, using the sides of both hands, pushing hard, trying to make them touch together while turning the dough piece in between. In doing this you should be stretching the outside surface and pushing it gently back through the centre, stretching every bubble as you go. You are now creating tension in the core of the dough piece, and to check for this internal tension, gently press on the top with one finger. If the process has been completed fully, it will spring back; if it not, then continue, but being careful not to start to tear the surface, which would cause you to pass from handing up back through to the development stage. This would start to destroy the cell structure created rather than extend the cells.

This process will take about 15 minutes to complete, so don't rush it, as it can be a very therapeutic and enjoyable part of the bread making experience. The dough pieces will quickly recover, and within 20 minutes or so, grow to the size it took 1 hour to achieve through the bulk proof. Working with this at this stage should help you to appreciate how quickly spores multiply once reintroduced to fresh foods, also the importance of this stage of the process.

If the dough has been set within the right parameters, you could add an extra intermediate proof in, helping you to move even closer to optimum fermentation. This will create a crisper crust and more oven spring. Each time you do this, it will gas up much more quickly, moving the dough closer and closer to the edge of being over-fermented if practised too many times. For now we will work with just the one intermediate proof, so you have a comparison; then once you have perfected this, you can start to play with this stage of the process, to learn and recognise its advantages.

Time to start processing the dough (make into the final shapes). For the finish of the cottage loaf you may wish to finish off with seeds; if so, you will need to make up some skilly wash for the right effect.

PITTA

Make sure your oven is on at the parameters set in the oven and baking paragraph. You will need a rolling pin; when referring to its use through the process, it will simply be pin. You will need to bring from under the bowl the two or three 50g units, depending on your choice of flour, and because we are going to pin these out very thin to an oval shape about 20cm by 10cm (8 by 4 inches), we will need to work on a generously-floured work surface to prevent them from sticking. To pin out, roll the dough piece around in the flour, ensuring it is fully coated, then using the palm of the hand, press down on it to expel the gas. Then take your rolling pin and start applying pressure evenly, rolling up and down only. Don't pin sideways, as this will form a circle, and the traditional pittas should be oval. Turn the piece over, ensuring it is still coated well with flour to prevent it sticking, and keep repeating until the correct dimensions are reached. This can take a little time to achieve, as it will continually want to shrink back. If you are having trouble, tease it halfway out, put it to one side while you work on the next one, then return to the first one. It will have quickly relaxed, making it easier to extend and retain the size you want.

When watching people on the workshops putting this into practice, I have noticed there is a tendency to hold the bottom end of the dough piece with the fingers of one hand while applying pressure with the rolling pin in the other. This method inevitably shrinks back. You are better to apply even downward pressure while rolling up and down until the shape is formed. If you have long finger nails, care should be taken not to pierce the shape with them, as this will cause a fracture, releasing the steam within the one big cell we are trying to create when placed into the oven.

The oval shapes then need to be thrown directly onto the hot tray that was placed in the oven when it was turned on. If you are concerned about burning yourself, use a simple piece of plywood or a tray without sides to slip it off. Large slips or peels are used in the industry for all oven bottom breads, making it a very efficient way to load a full chamber quickly.

Once in the oven, they take just seconds to blister as the moistures start to boil. This then creates steam; the cells within this small piece of dough can't take the pressure, so start to snap the cell walls, making them form one large cell. The outside surface, being nice and supple, continues to expand, creating a void through the centre, giving you perfect hollow pittas that will always open. As soon as this has completely opened they need to come out of the oven to ensure they will keep supple and not lose any more moisture than is necessary. Once cooled, they will keep this way for three or four days if kept in an airtight bag.

This bread is not only a very good way to encourage children to eat it, as it will appear to be magic to them if they see it taking place; it also helps to demonstrate the importance of a well-balanced dough. If you start to see a hollowing under the crust of your loaf or the crust falling away from the crumb, it will be a good indication that it is out of balance. This can probably be attributed to underproofing along the line somewhere. Just as we showed in these simple pitta breads, the strands will snap as the heat penetrates.

When we do catering, I often make these in just 20g to 25g units and pin them out to small rounds, then bake them at 180°C until they have opened and dried out. They are then stacked on the table in a pyramid for people to take and pop over their soup. It is not as heavy as a bread roll, which could be too much if eating many courses, but more like a crouton, and will always break the ice around the table as people start to pass them around to each other.

COTTAGE LOAF

You will need to clear the excess flour left over from the pittas from the workbench before you start work on the cottage loaf. Bring out the largest of the four pieces left under the bowl; it will be very lively now. To make the cottage loaf we need to chop this into two pieces, one piece being two-thirds the size of the other. No need to weigh it; random sizes will add to its individual personality.

Once divided, starting with the larger of the two pieces, you then need to give this its final mould. It should be as tight as you can get it without tearing, just as we have done on the previous moulds. Once you are happy you have created a nice tight ball, check the internal tension, using your finger on the top to make sure. If it's too slack, your head will sink into your shoulders once topped. Put this to one side with the seams to the bottom, preferably onto something coarse, such as semolina or ground rice. These are commonly used here, and in the south of France and parts of southern Italy, some use ground olive pips. Wow! What an add-on flavour. See if you can find them.

Repeat the moulding action with the smaller piece, ensuring it is as tight as you can make it, but don't set this one onto the semolina, just onto a clear work surface. If you get flour or semolina on the base of this one, there will be a danger that the head will not adhere to the base when we come to build the loaf, resulting in it falling off when baked. These will now rest while the three-strand plait is being moulded.

THREE STRAND PLAIT

You will have three dough pieces left under the bowl. Bring these forward ready to mould. The same principle of stretching the outside through the centre will be applied to these as with the round shape, but we are going to make each into an elongated sausage shape ready for the strands to build the plait.

Press out each piece using the palm of the hand to expel the gas, make sure it is free from the bench, then starting from the top, start folding over a little at a time, pushing it firmly without tearing into the piece directly beneath it.

Continue this along the top edge, working all the way along until you get to the other end. This action will need to be repeated until you reach the bottom edge, resulting in a nice tight elongated torpedo shape. Repeat this the other two.

When all three are completed, go back to the first one, as it will now have relaxed, making it more forgiving and less likely to shrink back through the fine mould. They want to be elongated to about 30cm (12 inches). This is done by using the full hand from the heel through to the fingertips, rolling backwards and forwards, starting from the middle of the dough piece and using both hands, slowly working your way out through to the ends. Each time you move out, apply a little more pressure against the bench, gently squeezing the gas from the cells as you work your way out. This should result in a nice even taper towards each end.

BUILDING THE PLAIT

Take all three strands and place them with the tapers coming directly down toward you, pinch them tightly together at the top, making sure they are all free from the work surface and spread well apart when doing so. Then to plait them, it is best to look on it as if you have a left outside strand, a middle strand, and a right outside strand. Taking the right outside strand, you will bring it over the middle strand; this then will become the middle strand. Then taking the left outside strand, bring this over the middle strand, making this now the middle strand. This pattern is now repeated all the way down, right over the middle, left over the middle, and so on, until you reach the bottom, creating a neat uniform plait with a nice bulbous middle, gently tapering off towards each end.

Once completed, place on a semolina base and lightly dust with flour (no need to cover). The final proof on this loaf will only be about 15 minutes, guaranteeing plenty of action through the centre of the outside crust, creating a lovely burst. This can only be achieved with confidence because you have taken the trouble to set the dough within the controls. We now know the cells are nice and relaxed, and we have a whole army of yeast spores ready to give their all on their final fling before they are killed off with the heat. The sponge and knock backs have brought us as close to optimum fermentation as we can get, even in this short processing time.

BUILDING THE COTTAGE LOAF

While the plait is proving, you have the time to prep the cottage loaf. Bring forward the larger of the two pieces, making sure that there is sufficient semolina underneath to keep it free flowing and not sticking to the bench. Pick up the smaller piece, and just run the scraper underneath to free it from the bench, as it may be a little tacky on the bottom. Place this centrally on the top of the large one, then with two fingers, be brave and plunge them down through both pieces, from the top right through until you can feel the work surface. Once you can feel it, just give a little tweak outwards at the bottom to ensure you weld the top to the bottom. Bring your fingers out, turn the whole loaf through ninety degrees and repeat, to ensure the loaf is nice and symmetrical.

If you wish to top with seeds, then the skilly wash will need to have been prepared. Take this and, with a paint brush, paint sparingly all the way over the outside, then finish off by sprinkling with seeds of your choice. A blend of poppy and sesame with a few black onion seeds is a good combination.

Once completed, you need to score lightly with a sharp knife 6 or 8 times all the way around the edge, cutting down from top to bottom. Too deep and the loaf will flow as you will release too much tension; not deep enough, there will be a danger the head will jump and fall off when the loaf leaps into action through the bake. Because of the time the dough balls sat before the loaf was built, also the time allocated to the final preparation of the loaf, once cut, this can then go straight into the oven.

The plait will also be ready to bake at the same time, but they will both need to have steam added to the chamber. When you turned your oven on, you should have placed a thick baking tray about a third of the way up on the rack. You should also have placed a shallow baking tin with sides right at the very bottom of the chamber. Both now should be as hot as they can be. Get half a cup of cold water ready within easy reach of the oven. Off we go: place both loaves into the chamber on to the hot tray one third up, taking care to ensure they are spaced well apart to avoid them touching as they grow. Pick up the half a cup of cold water and throw into the hot shallow baking pan at the bottom and close the door quickly.

Most small 400g loaves will only take about 22 minutes to bake. After this, it is purely cosmetic and personal preference. If you like them lightly baked and are concerned that they might not be fully baked, then use your temperature probe to spear the core of the loaf before you take it out. If it reaches 94°C to 96°C, it will be fully baked, regardless of the external colour. If you like them darker and crisper, then leave them longer and maybe reduce the heat by 10 degrees for the last 10 minutes of the bake. You could even open the door for 30 seconds to draw off any excess steam still in the chamber, to help complement the crust retention; you are in control.

When fully baked, these breads should stand at an ambient temperature to cool down, preferably not directly onto a cold surface such as marble or granite worktops. The two extremes will create moisture, encouraging the crust to soften. A wire rack or wooden chopping board, a tea towel or even cardboard will be fine. As the product starts to cool, it will sing to you as the surface starts to crack, creating a lovely tortoiseshell appearance to the crust. If the edges of this effect curl slightly as they separate, this is a good indication you have reached optimum fermentation through the process. The temptation will be to hack into it as soon as it has come out of the oven but it will need the respect of a couple of hours to cool down to fully appreciate the flavours and textures your hard work has created.

SODA BREADS

I slip this one in as it is a quick and easy loaf to produce, so even the busiest of us can make it. Once you get into the habit of producing them, you could have bread on the table ready to eat in 45 minutes from start to finish. It is a good starting point to encourage children to work with breads, as it gives instant results and is nice and messy to handle. It is a different way of aerating a product to fermentation. We will be relying on natural ingredients to react when introduced to each other, creating gas to lighten the texture. We will be moving to the other end of the development programme compared to the first dough we made. We don't want to encourage the functional glutens to develop on this one, so it will be folded rather than developed. It has no yeast, so if you find you have a yeast intolerance, this is the place to start.

This bread is very versatile and underestimated. When it first crossed over the water from Ireland to be placed onto the supermarket shelves, it was poorly represented in the quest to mass-produce this simple bread. Traditionally it is made from the soft Irish flour, then just the minimum of ingredients such as buttermilk, bicarbonate of soda and salt are added, to be gently folded together before being thrown on a hot griddle over a peat fire or the sole of an oven.

What evolved in mass production was the result of a problem in obtaining large quantities of buttermilk, a simple by-product of making butter. This ingredient was used for its natural acidity, which activates the bicarbonate of soda. When milk and baking powder were used as a substitute, the cream of tartar in the bicarbonate of soda, used to activate it, left a less than desirable after taste. The product was then put into planetary mixers to mix for speed and convenience, resulting in the functional glutens naturally toughening up in the flour. To counteract this, fats or oils would be added to isolate some of the functional glutens, moving it closer to a scone texture rather than a soda bread. In some cases I have seen engineered dough relaxants used because of a lack of understanding of this simple bread. Through working in Ireland with many small producers of this bread, it was very apparent some of the best were always mixed by hand in a folding action, rather than the aggressive development needed for fermentation.

It is very versatile loaf that can be enjoyed when produced with just the four ingredients: flour, salt, bicarbonate of soda, buttermilk. It can also carry almost any additional ingredient as well. Try Stilton and walnut, or grated Bramley apple and Cheddar cheese, before you start on the obvious olive and sundried tomato that are so fashionable now. For demonstration purposes we will be adding sunflower seeds and feta cheese and a few mixed herbs. This is a good example of how different reactions take place when blending ingredients. The natural oils in the sunflower seeds, when put with bicarbonate of soda and buttermilk, will change to a delicate shade of green, once baked and exposed to the atmosphere. This will also happen with linseed. Feta cheese will not melt, as will the Stilton and Cheddar, resulting in a good presentation of the loaf, with the green flecks of the sunflower seeds and the white of the feta chunks creating a fascination needed to attract people to this simple bread.

When producing this bread, there is a simple reaction that goes on between the buttermilk and the bicarbonate of soda, creating a gas as soon as these two ingredients are put together. This is controllable to a certain extent by ensuring you work with cool ingredients. This helps to retard this activity a little, but it is advisable for you to have your oven on and up to temperature, with a solid tray one third up in the oven, hot and ready to emulate the sole of a traditional oven before you start. If the mixture is allowed to gas up too much before the bake, it will be detrimental to the final crumb structure, as it can only gas once.

The salt added to this product will do nothing other than to bring taste to it, so if you wish you may adjust to a comfortable level for you, without affecting the finished article's performance.

The blend of flour can be of your choice. I have found the southern Ireland flours are what they call wheaten; this is predominantly the endosperm (white particles) with about 20% bran added. The Northern Ireland loaf is produced with mainly very coarse wholemeal flours. Try using a blend of 50% white flour, 30% wholemeal and 20% wheat germ or oats, to make the 100%; this is a good combination. For this recipe we will be blending two thirds wholemeal and one third white to make your 100%; this works well.

We are going to fold this dough by hand and it will get messy, so when you weigh out your flour it is advisable to allocate a generous handful of flour onto the work surface, ready to place the dough onto it when you scoop it out of the bowl after blending. This will help you to be able to come free from it when you are all stuck up, hopefully!

In the equation, the amount of bicarbonate of soda will work out to 7.5g; don't get hung up on the 0.5, just round it down to seven.

Buttermilk is more readily available in most health food shops and on the supermarket shelves now. If you can find the live buttermilk, it has a better taste and is obviously better for you. The tub sizes do vary from a convenient 250g tub through to 300g. I have found the 300g tubs are not live, and therefore a little thicker, so you are able to use them in their entirety. If you can't find the true buttermilk, then the live bio yogurt is a better substitute. Just let it down with 10% milk, which will bring it to the right consistency. I have in the past used soya milk with a squeeze of lemon juice, for those suffering with a lactose intolerance. This logic will also apply to plain milk, but you will need to leave this overnight in the fridge to get the right activity.

SODA BREAD

INGREDIENTS	%	GRAMS
Flour	100	250
Salt	2	5
Bicarbonate of soda	3	7
Herbs	to taste	to taste
Buttermilk	100	250
Feta cheese cubed	30	75
Sunflower seeds	25	62
	Total	649

METHOD

Place a generous handful of wholemeal flour on the workbench, ready to coat the sticky dough in when you've finished blending it.

Into a large bowl weigh the flour, salt, bicarbonate of soda, all together, and rub well through to make sure all the small ingredients are well distributed.

Add the herbs and sunflower seeds and blend well once again.

Add the feta cubes and just gently roll them around in the flour to ensure they are separated and evenly coated with flour but not crumbled.

Take the buttermilk, making sure the lid is still secured (there are some funny stories in the workshop with this one if it isn't), and give it a good shake before emptying the contents of the tub on top of the ingredients blended in the bowl.

Then using one hand to hold the bowl, use the other hand slightly cupped to gently fold by continually bringing the dry ingredients from the bottom, rotating the bowl as you go, ensuring they are all coated with the liquids. Keep gently folding until there isn't any visible flour or liquid exposed and the dough has formed a rough-looking texture sitting in the bowl. (You need to be brave now.) With one movement scoop up as much of the dough as you can in one hand from the bottom of the bowl and bring it across to the pile of flour on the work bench. Place it gently on top to keep it free from the bench, then clean up the bowl and hands and tack any stray pieces of dough onto the exposed sticky surface of the dough. When you are happy all is incorporated, proceed to picking up the dough and rolling it around in the dry flour until fully coated on the outside, but try not to fold any of the dry flour into the core of the loaf, as this can sometimes change the texture of the finished article. You should just have enough time to clean yourself up before prepping the loaf ready for the oven.

Your oven is up to temperature, your thick baking sheet or stone is in the oven as hot as it can be. Take your slip (thin piece of ply or baking sheet without sides) and sprinkle it liberally with semolina or something coarse, just wholemeal flour will be sufficient if nothing else is readily available. Place the dough piece onto the slip, ensuring it is spinning freely from the surface, then, using a scraper or knife, cut into four equal-sized pieces to create the shape associated with this traditional bread.

I was told by a lovely old Irish lady when she was teaching me as we sat around a very smoky peat fire with eyes streaming, the breads were cut in this way to let the leprechauns out. I think it may be to help the heat penetrate the core of the loaf more efficiently, but it's still a story I love to remember her for, and the wonderful way these people have of telling a story, making it believable. Once ready, slip the loaf directly into the oven onto the hot baking surface you have created and close the door.

This bread will only take about 17 minutes to bake; after this it will be purely cosmetic as to how you like your breads to be. I must admit I prefer this bread to be a little on the dark and crunchy side, but if you like it to be soft and are unsure if it is baked, use the probe to ensure you reach the magic 94°C to 96°C core temperature (you are in control). Bake it as you like it.

Once baked, give it the respect of about 30 minutes to cool before eating. Once fully cooled, it can be stored in the fridge in a bag for a week or more.

ENRICHED DOUGH

This dough is to demonstrate the use of natural dough enhancers such as sugar and fats. If you look at the base ingredients, they will be the same as the very first bread dough: 100% flour, 2% salt, 2% yeast, and water; the only additions to that will be sugar to flavour and butter to soften. These amounts can vary according to the name of the product; for instance, brioche, having reduced sugar and much higher fat content, down to a scone with a minimum of both and aerated in the same way as the soda breads. This recipe is used for a whole range of sweet morning goods in the industry in the UK, and more should be done to resurrect them, as they are probably healthier because of the lower fat content than the continental products such as Danish pastry's 40% butter and brioche's 50% butter that we have come to accept as a treat.

This dough could make Chelsea buns, currant buns, Bath buns, tea cakes, and many others, even our traditional doughnuts before the influence of the American doughnut, full of strange things to make them represent a puff ball. The only difference is the shape and how you add dried fruits and spices. The important part of this recipe is not what we make with it but how the dough is put together. Sugar, fat, spice, and even the oils they coat the dried fruits with to keep them free flowing are all retardants (which kill yeast spores) so we must ensure that the yeasts added are well on their way to multiplying before we introduce these ingredients to them. These products have many rich flavours of their own, and the whole product range will be encouraged to have a soft eating crust, so there is little point in adding concentrated fermentation in the form of an overnight sponge to help with the stability, as we did with the crusty breads at the start.

So I will now be encouraging you to work with a flying sponge, aptly named because of the speed it works at. When it is set down in the batter form, it takes just 40 to 50 minutes to reach a peak before falling back. When this has happened, its job is done; it is now in a hurry to be introduced to the remainder of the flour to feast on. This is a way of ensuring the yeasts multiply readily, making them stable before being influenced by retardants, and it is normally put into practice for anything soft eating. It will also help you to appreciate the speed yeasts spores will multiply themselves at, quickly depleting the food readily available without the influence of salt, if the batter is left to reproduce on its own without you intervening.

When it has dropped, it falls back naturally and reintroduces itself to fresh foods. This can happen about three times over about a 2 to 2½ hour period. Each time this happens, it will find new foods to feast on, creeping back up the bowl, and speeding up every time it recovers. This action will get quicker and quicker until it finally has nothing left to encourage it to multiply, so it will give up and die. This would happen in the main dough if salt were not applied to a controlled level.

This should help you to understand the importance of accurate salt addition to the breads, as well as the many different methods to make breads using this fact for its advantages. You can quickly add speed and flavour to a ferment using the delayed salt method, as well as flying sponge, which is generally used when using softer flours such as all-English grist flours, when you won't have the tolerances of the harder wheats incorporated to extend the longer ferments also often practised in traditional products such as French breads.

You could also lend this method to the very first basic breads, using those lovely sweet-flavoured English wheats, instead of concentrated overnight sponges. Set the flyer, add to the main dough without the salt addition, roughly develop; give this just 30 minutes' bulk fermentation before adding the salt. Add this and continue to develop until silky smooth. Follow this by giving it 1 hour's bulk fermentation, then process as with the method for the cottage range of breads. If only given the one knock back, it will not have the intense crusts associated with the overnight sponge, but if you practise knocking back every 15 minutes a couple of times, you can get it to emulate these characteristics as you push it closer to optimum fermentation (once again you are in control).

The recipe that follows will be the 100% of the ingredients, but don't weigh them all into one bowl, as we will be splitting them to ensure the dough is built in the right way. The flying sponge will be set down first, then the remainder of the ingredients will be weighed separately into another bowl. The full recipe is set out to help you appreciate the similarities to the very first bread dough produced to make the cottage loaf and so on.

BASE RECIPE FOR ENRICHED DOUGH		
INGREDIENTS	%	GRAMS
White flour	100	500
Salt	2	10
Yeast	2	10
Sugar	15	75
Butter	15	75
Water	54	270
	Total	940

The amount of flying sponge set down can vary from product to product, dependent on sweet or savoury and texture required. For this range we will be using 40% of our flour in the flying sponge, all of the yeast and all of the water. The water will need to be set at the right temperature to bring this part of the dough to the magic 28°C; doing this will ensure control at the very important start of the dough's life. Yes, this part of the dough will cool a little as it sits around for 40 or so minutes at ambient temperature, but this will prove to you the importance of releasing the yeasts at the correct temperature. Then once they are well on their way to multiplying, they are difficult to stop, even if the dough temperature drops a little, and we throw retardants such as fat and sugar at them; they just keep growing.

FLYING SPONGE		
Take from the above ingredients and put into a bowl large enough to cope with it more than doubling in size before it falls back		
INGREDIENTS	%	GRAMS
Flour	40	200
Yeast	100	10
Water tempered	100	270

This is then beaten to a smooth batter, and I would recommend you do this using your hand rather than a spoon or fork to start with, so you can feel its texture. If you then repeat this procedure when you return to it after the time allocated, you will feel the difference in the consistency and the cell structure, which will help you to understand the importance of this small part of the dough in the procedure, and why it is needed. Set this to one side for 40 to 50 minutes or until it drops. Once it has closed itself down, it is an indication the spores are searching for new foods.

While this is taking place, weigh the all the remaining ingredients, with exception of the butter, into another large bowl. The butter being isolated is a critical fact, and why so many enriched recipes, such as hot cross buns, fall short of your expectations of the results, as suggested by the photos in many recipe books. This has thankfully kept me employed for many hours, answering the same disappointed emails from many people.

The butter will need to be kept separate from the main dough until the flour is fully hydrated and the moisture has all been encouraged to make the functional glutens nice and elastic. Once this has happened, you can add the butter around the outside of this structure without any fear of entering the pastry or scone stage, which is when we will utilise the fats at the other end of the spectrum to create the bite we are looking for.

MAIN ENRICHED DOUGH

INGREDIENTS	%	GRAMS
Flour	100	300
Salt	3.5	10
Sugar, fine	25	75
Butter	25	75
Flying sponge	150* entire flying sponge	450
	Total	910

*Some of the weight in the flying sponge will have been lost through evaporation as fermentation has taken place. There is also residue left around the bowl, no matter how hard you try to scrape it clean, resulting in roughly 450g being available to add to the main dough.

When the flyer has dropped, it is time to build the dough. Before you start, take note of the cell structure. It will be large and open, popping and bubbling of its own accord. Now run your fingers through it just as you did when blending it at the start. You will now feel a resilience within this batter, proving how this small act can strengthen this part of the dough, but also as you run your fingers through, the cells will split, creating many more small cells. Each will have its own spore, thus multiplying this army to help cope with the ingredients it will have thrown at it later on in its life.

Now add this to the bowl with the above flour, salt and sugar, and continue to bring together in the normal way until roughly forming a rugged dough, then out onto the bench to continue the development as with the previous white dough. At this stage the dough will be very tight and it will take a bit of muscle to get it to tear, but this will be necessary to ensure that the gluten strands are developed before the butter is applied. Once you are happy there is elasticity within this part of the dough, you can then add the butter and continue to squeeze and tear. It will be a little messy, but trust me, the butter will eventually disappear, being incorporated into the dough, forming a lovely soft silky feel to the dough. Rest it for a couple of minutes, then continue to develop further for a couple of minutes just to make sure. Dust the bottom of the bowl liberally with flour, then place the dough piece in. Once in, dust the top of the dough piece liberally with flour to ensure it falls out of the bowl without having to tear it out after the bulk proof period, giving a nice uniform shape to start processing, then cover the bowl.

If adding the butter in a mixer using a dough hook, it is advisable to add it in small portions, making sure each piece is well mixed in before adding the next, as it will keep jumping out of the bowl if added in one lump.

This dough will be comfortable with 1 to 1½ hour bulk fermentation if being used as a plain dough with fruits added externally such as Chelsea buns or Bath buns, but if the fruits and spices are to be incorporated internally, for currant buns, tea cakes, hot cross buns, fruit loaves and so on, I would recommend the dough is allowed to bulk ferment for about 15 minutes to ensure the yeast activity has recovered from the addition of fats and sugars. Then tear in the fruits and spices; this will ensure you get a lighter textured finished article. Add them too soon, and everything will slow down, putting the dough out of balance.

HOT CROSS BUNS

After 15 minutes' bulk proof, tear in the following ingredients based on the 100% flour we started out with in the recipe, in this case it was 500g.

INGREDIENTS	%	GRAMS
Mixed spice	3	15
This would be added and mixed in clear		
Currants	15	75
Sultanas	15	75
Mixed peel	5	25
*Zest of lemon and orange		

*Zest of lemon and orange if you have time and you can set the fruit the night before with the zest in it; this will then marinate, giving the full advantage of these flavours.

This blend of fruits is torn into the dough as evenly as possible before the dough is placed back into the bowl to complete the bulk fermentation process.

After the bulk proof, the dough is scaled into 80g units, moulded to a nice tight round ball and placed on the work bench under an upturned bowl, to prevent them from forming a skin, for a 15 minute intermediate proof. They are then remoulded and placed on a baking sheet, ensuring there is plenty of space between for them to grow. Once again, these will benefit from having their final proof under a plastic bowl or in a plastic bag to retain the moisture given off, keeping them nice and supple, and helping them to grow evenly. If kept in these conditions, the final proof should only be about 40 minutes.

CROSSING MIX		
INGREDIENTS	%	GRAMS
White flour	100	100
Salt	4	4
Water	90	90
Oil	20	20
	Total	214

Place the flour and salt into a bowl, add 60% of the water and beat to a clear thick batter. Add the remaining water a little at a time, ensuring the mixture is lump free each time you add it, then fold in the oil to form a smooth free-running batter of a piping consistency. This is piped on the surface of the bun using a fine plain piping tube and a savoy bag (piping bag, made of cloth or disposable plastic). Just before they are baked, the oven should be pre-heated and set at 190°C to 200°C . The bake should only be 12 minutes. As soon as they come out of the oven, wash with a thin syrup wash, consisting of 2 parts of sugar to 1 part of water, just brought to the boil.

CURRANT BUNS

To produce a simple currant bun the same procedure is used, but no spice is added and 30% of the flour weight in currants is the only fruit torn in. Each unit is still weighed in at 80g, moulded to a nice tight round shape, and given 15 minutes' intermediate proof before remoulding to a nice tight round shape again, proved and baked as for the hot cross buns.

TEA CAKE

This product has a little spice added, just 1% to 1.5% of the flour weight, and it is much lighter in the fruit content, normally just 15% of the flour weight, traditionally just currants. This is then weighed into 100g units, moulded to a nice tight round shape, and given a 15 minute intermediate proof before pinning out to a 10cm disk (four inches). These are placed on a baking sheet so that they are just touching, and lightly docked (pricked) before baking, using a fork to prevent blistering just under the surface crust when baked. The proof and bake time will be as with the buns; these can be washed over with a little beaten egg before the bake or washed with the syrup wash after the bake.

BATH BUNS

The traditional Bath bun is rarely found now. Even the ones sold in Bath are a poor imitation of it in its true form. They are slightly richer and have glacé cherries and egg, and are topped with sugar nibs before baking.

The fruit is chopped in rather than torn in and it should be of a rough chopped appearance, piled in 80g pyramids, with a generous sprinkling of the sugar nibs on the top.

FRUIT BLEND BASED ON THE FLOUR WEIGHT

INGREDIENTS	%	GRAMS
Currants	15	75
Sultanas	10	50
Raisins	10	50
Mixed peel	7	35
Glacé cherries	10	50
Zest of a lemon and orange to marinate		
1 egg		

Sugar nibs: these are difficult to find for domestic use, so if you can find the coarse preserving sugar, this will suffice, but be careful not to confuse it with the fine jam making sugar.

BUILDING THE BATH BUN

After the dough has had its bulk fermentation time, tip out onto the work surface and knock back by pressing to expel the gas, then just simply fold the bottom third to the middle, the top third over the middle and bottom, turn it over so the seam is to the bottom and cover with the bowl for 15 minutes' intermediate proof. When the time has passed, take off the bowl and press the dough out flat, add the fruit blend on the top of this dough and then crack the egg over the top. With a scraper, proceed to chop the fruit and egg in, continually bringing in the bits from around the edges, making sure you keep a rough and rugged coarse texture. The liquid egg will make sure they don't join together. Once happy that you have the right texture, break off rough pieces weighing 80g and pile in neat pyramid shapes, well-spaced on a lined baking tray. Once again, prove under cover for just 30 minutes. These need to be baked under-proved rather than over, to help them retain that chunky appearance. Before setting into the oven, pile a generous amount of the sugar nibs on top and place into the oven. A light bake will be beneficial to this product. When they come out, give them a light wash with the syrup wash.

CHELSEA BUNS

To build this product is slightly different. To make the traditional Chelsea bun, you will need mixed spice, about 50g of softened butter and 30% of the initial flour weight in currants (150g), also 80g of fine sugar, soft brown is nice in this product, and a rolling pin. A little egg wash is good if you have it readily available but don't waste an egg; a splash of water or milk will seal the ends just as well. You also need a wash brush. Once processed it will be baked in a lined frame or baking pan with sides measuring 20cm by 25cm (about 8 inches by 10 inches). If you can't find one, make a wooden frame to these dimensions.

When I was serving as an apprentice, all dried fruits and fats would be delivered in thin wooden boxes. These would then be used for many things in the bakery, especially for cake frames for the slab cake range, but also for products such as Chelsea buns, sister brick loaves, reinvented in today's world as batch breads, and the quarterns, a 4lb or 1600g loaf made for the hotel and catering trade. This would be baked in a wooden frame, as this would help the sides of the loaf stay soft and lightly baked, wood being a good insulator. They would then be taken to the customer for them to slice in-house on a special wooden frame to ensure regular slice width. All these products needed support to make them in their traditional shape. In my early days in the bakery, the boxes were used for me to stand on so that I could reach the handle on the tart blocker, or sit on around the back of the fridge cracking out thousands of suspicious looking eggs. These box frames would be used continually, year after year. Wood was a regularly-used retainer, but it has been forgotten; why not bring it back?

Tip the dough out onto a lightly floured work surface. It should come out in a nice neat ball, as the bowl was floured before it was set down for the bulk proof. Pull out four corners, creating a rough square, then using a rolling pin, pin up and down to form a rectangle 35cm down and 25cm (about 14 by 10 inches) across. You may need to keep turning the dough over to keep it free from the work bench when rolling out. Once the size has been achieved, wash the bottom 2cm (1 inch) or so with egg, milk, or water to help form a seal later. The remaining surface will be brushed liberally with the softened (not melted) butter, making sure you keep a little back for use later, then sprinkled liberally with the fine sugar, followed by a generous sprinkling of the mixed spice, finally spread the dried fruit all over, making sure the moist 2cm at the bottom is still exposed.

Now it can get a little tricky; you are going to roll this down starting from the top, stretching and rolling a little at a time as you go, to try to keep it the same even shape all the way down. This often wants to get wider and wider as you work your way down until you get used to handling it, creating an enormous croissant shape. You won't be the first, and it isn't the end of the world if this does happen. Once sealed at the bottom on the sticky bit, just push your fingers up through the centre of each end to get it back to the 25 to 30cm width originally set out.

These buns are going to be set into the baking pan or frame very close together, so as they prove they will push against each other, encouraging something that goes in round to become the square shape associated with the Chelsea bun. Naturally if something is baked this close together, they will weld to each other, resulting in them having to be cut apart, making them ugly in appearance when finished. To prevent this from happening, we will use our ingredients once again by painting the whole of the outside surface with the remaining butter. Once coated, both the top and bottom all the way around, it will need to be divided into 12 equal-sized pieces. It may be better to mark them out before you cut, to ensure you have just twelve. Mark the middle, then mark the middle of those two pieces; you will now have four pieces. Then if you mark twice in each quarter, this will result in three equal-sized pieces in each quarter. Times these by four makes twelve.

I hope this translates better in the written word than around the table. I have seen from eight to fifteen cut, and only twelve will fit in the frame, so very often there are buns being passed around to make the numbers up. This will be difficult on your own. Once you have your twelve, these will then be turned onto their side and placed into the frame, 3 across the short side and 4 down the long side, with the swirl facing up towards you. Gently push down to help push them against each other and place under cover for the final proof of 1 hour. The bake is about 20 to 25 minutes.

The normal finish on these is the syrup wash, then a sprinkle of caster sugar, but I do prefer the Danish pastry finish of crystallised icing sugar. This can be achieved by mixing a little icing sugar and water to make a thick paste, adding a little almond essence and warming to just above blood heat over boiling water or in the microwave for a few seconds. This will make it thin and runny, then when the buns come out and while they are still hot, brush this liberally over the top surface. This will quickly crystallise, creating a lovely crunchy sweet topping. Once cooled and taken from the frame, each bun should separate easily from the others, creating a silky soft side with a nice caramelised top and bottom.

This method is very versatile and can carry any addition. Try cinnamon and grated cooking apple, chocolate buttons are a favourite with the grandchildren, or lemon curd and ground roasted hazelnuts. At Christmas time you can create a Christmas crown by adding ground almonds, dried cranberries and chopped marzipan. Cut into 14 equal-sized pieces and place 7 of them into each of two 20cm sponge pans, putting 1 in the middle and 6 around the outside. As they prove up and bake, they will splay out over the edge, creating a crown appearance when baked. This is then dusted heavily with icing sugar before presentation; it's much better and simpler than Stollen.

SHORT CRUST PASTRY

This is the final product produced on the basic workshop. This will take you right to the other end of the spectrum using just the one type of flour. The very first dough was created using the functional glutens to their full potential to retain the gases given off through the fermentation process for as long as possible.

In the second dough set to make the soda bread, we didn't want this to happen and we had no other ingredient that we could add without changing the characteristics of the final loaf. We then folded the dough rather than stretching and tearing, preventing the glutens from becoming stretchy as they hydrated. If they had, they would have restricted the limited action of gassing that takes place when the bicarbonate of soda and buttermilk react when introduced to the heat in the oven.

In the third dough (the enriched dough) we wanted to create this elasticity within the base dough once again to retain the gases through the fermentation process. We also wanted to add sugar at very high levels as a flavouring, without slowing things down. This was overcome by using the flying sponge as a method to help get the yeasts over the first hurdle. We also added high levels of fats to this in such a way that they wouldn't influence the extensibility of the dough, ending up in them being added to bring softness and flavour to the dough, using them purely as an enhancer rather than a shortener, as with a scone or pastry.

The fourth mix takes you right to the other end of the baking spectrum, making a short pastry that will never shrink back, resulting in the filling spewing out, no matter how many times you re-use the scraps. It will not need to filled with baking beans to prevent it from blistering when baked blind, and should never give you a soggy bottom if not blind baked before filling with liquid fillings, such as custard tart on a sweet or quiche on a savoury pastry.

There are lots of advantages, but this pastry still uses the same white flour as for all the other products, to encourage you to question the addition of each ingredient, and when they need to be added when working from your favourite recipe book.

This pastry will be taking shortness to the extreme but at least this should help you understand what is going on, so if you prefer the rub-in method given in most recipe books, you know why you are rubbing the fats into the flour. It is to coat as many of the small particles of the flour with the fat as you possibly can, helping to create a barrier all around the outside of each of the particles, so preventing the moistures from penetrating. This will help to stop them from becoming elastic. Any particles exposed will naturally hydrate; that is why, especially through the winter when all the ingredients are cold, it can take longer to rub the fats around these individual particles, but if you rub for your normal time, your pastry will demand higher hydration, making it more elastic. Any elasticity within pastry will cause shrinkage. This will also become magnified each time you gather it up to re–roll.

This method also works if you want the pastry to be partly elastic, say for a Cornish pasty, short to the bite but just elastic enough to be able to crimp the edges. You can decide to what point to rub the fat into the flour; the finer you rub it, the shorter it will be to the bite, once again putting you in control of something as simple as a short crust pastry.

SHORT SWEET PASTRY		
INGREDIENTS	%	GRAMS
White flour	100	200
Butter	50	100
Fine white sugar	25	50
Water for short pastry	12.5	25
Egg if for sweet pastry		
	Total	375

METHOD

Weigh the butter, sugar and liquid into the bowl, then cream together. Once again, it may be better to use your fingertips to start with, so you can feel it as it starts to stiffen up and stick to the side of the bowl as the ingredients slowly become fully emulsified. When this has happened, there should be no moisture visible.

Add the flour and rub through until it forms a ball, clearing the sides of the bowl. When this has happened, you are safe to tip it out onto the work surface and start grinding it down to create a smooth pliable plasticized-like texture. It is impossible to overwork this, so don't worry, get it to a nice smooth texture.

It will be more user-friendly if it is allowed to settle down for 1 hour at room temperature if you want to use it the same day, or you could make a large batch and just keep it covered in the fridge, so when you need it, you can pinch off what you want, bring it out and soften it down by working on the bench before processing.

Another advantage will be at Christmas: to make the mince pies, line the base with the pastry as it is, then for the lids, scoop up the scraps, blend in a little baking powder and mix well together. It will still be short and pliable even after the second mix, but when baked, the lids will have a much lighter bite to them, with the base having lovely crisp but firm texture that won't crumble to the touch. (You are in control!)

SAVOURY PASTRY		
INGREDIENTS	%	GRAMS
White flour	100	200
Salt	1	2
Lard	25	50
Butter	25	50
Water	17	34
	Total	336

METHOD

The method for the savoury will be a little different, as it is more difficult to emulsify the liquid with the fat without the aid of the sugar. It is advisable to place the fat, salt, and just 25% of the flour into the bowl first, mash these up to form a paste, fully coating all the flour particles with the fat, then add the water to make the creamy batter. Once fully emulsified, add the remainder of the flour and carry on mixing until smooth.

"Clive is the most enthusiastic, dedicated and charming person. His passion for and knowledge about Real Bread shine through and touches everyone he teaches."

Alison Swan Parente, The Welbeck Bakehouse

"This is truly an exceptional bread course: informative, inspirational and rewarding. Clive Mellum is a very gentle, unassuming and modest man, but clearly outstanding at what he does, with a natural talent for conveying the minutiae of science, craftsmanship and care, all part of the baker's essential skill base."

Silvana de Soissons, The Foodie Bugle Shop, Bath

"Thank you, Clive, I had a brilliant day today. It is a long time since I have met someone as passionate about their trade and as knowledgeable as you."

Gary

Advanced Workshop

This range will encourage you to venture out a little as you start to develop your own skills. All the basic rules practiced through the basic range will still need to be applied, but by now it should be second nature to you, giving you more time to concentrate on experimenting a little more.

The Mother will be used as a yeast source, so you may need to think a week or so ahead to get the Mother up and running, if you are not already using her. You will need both the Rye Mother and the White Mother bubbling away, raring to go.

100% SOURDOUGH

This product is normally set to perform in the limited time we have in a workshop so that people can see the whole process right through. This is done by blending flours to help complement the faster process. The high percentage of the Mother dough is also added to assist in speeding things up, then the same logic is applied of folding to multiply these basic spores through the process. Doing it this way, you can get used to handling it and watching its progress through the day, as you make the bread. This will create a satisfactory loaf, but there are many, many different ways to build these doughs, this being one of the shortest.

When you are working away from home, you may not be able to dedicate the 4 hours or so necessary to tend to the whims of one dough. Often, as in the bakery, it will be more convenient to set the dough in the evening with much lower percentages of the Mother, then let it get on with it in the corner of the kitchen while you are asleep or out partying, depending on your age. I will give both methods to get you started, so you can start to tailor your recipe to suit your lifestyle.

The blend of flour is predominantly white flour, with wholemeal added for texture, flavour, and the colour associated with the ancient flours traditionally used to make these breads. Rye flour is added in small amounts as a relaxant to help to open the crumb, creating more oven spring and that cosmetically pleasing oven burst expected from these breads.

All sour doughs are more comfortable having their final proof in something that supports them, as there is a tendency for them to want to flow out, especially the rye. You don't need to go the great expense of what is now an overpriced traditional continental basket; a cheap wicker basket with a tea towel or a bowl with a tea towel will suffice; or just wrap it up in a well dusted tea towel. Wicker baskets have traditionally been used because, as the wood is dry and hungry for moisture, and the doughs give off moisture through the final proof stage, the wood tries to pull this through into itself. The heavy dusting of flour in between soaks up these moistures, so that when the loaf is turned out just before baking, all those important moistures containing lovely flavours aren't lost, they are all on the top of the loaf, helping to gelatinise the surface starches through the bake.

This type of dough will benefit from being as slack as you can handle it when you first put it down, as it tightens up through the fermentation process. The water content in the final dough will be dependent on the consistency of the Mother dough, as it is being added at such high proportions, so more discretion will be needed at the first stages of its life when developing the dough, and this is a skill you should now have started to implement when setting any dough down (you are in control, not the recipe).

As with all well balanced doughs, this will carry any additional seeds or dried fruit if they are added after the development stage, but if dry seeds are being added, then the dough will need to be set with higher water absorption to counteract the moistures soaked up by the seeds through the fermentation process.

A few suggestions that work well with this: one would be walnut and raisin. If you can find the Australian Lexia raisins, they are well worth the expense. Sunflower and soaked wheat or toasted bran with just a hint of cinnamon, or toasted nigella (black onion) and sesame seeds really work well together.

SOUR DOUGH SHORT PROCESS		
INGREDIENTS	%	GRAMS
White flour	80	400
Wholemeal flour	15	75
Medium rye flour	5	25
	Total	500
Salt	2	10
White mother*	50	250
Water	58	290 when starting out
	Total	1050

*Mother should have been fed at least 12 hours prior to being set into the main dough, to get her full benefit.

Finished dough temperature needs to be at the top end of the spectrum, 28°C when the dough is set. You may need to make a note of the first couple of doughs' finished temperatures to achieve this, then you can adjust slightly on the next run if necessary. There is a large amount of Mother going into each dough, and the Mother temperature will vary according to your ambient temperature on the day. Normally she will be running at the same temperature as the flour, so adding just 5°C to the finished water temperature will be sufficient, but it is well worth tracking this one to make sure the dough starts out right (good practice).

METHOD

Place all of the ingredients into the bowl in one go and bring to a rough dough. Once it is fully hydrated, tip out onto the workbench to travel through the development process. These doughs will develop relatively quickly compared to the doughs using brewer's yeast. They will have so much more concentrated acidity in the Mother dough being introduced to them. This will start to work on the strands quickly, so you will definitely benefit from mixing for a short while, resting for a while, mixing for a short while, and resting and so on, until it clears the bench. It will be more tacky than the dough using brewer's yeast, and it may be a little difficult for you to get away from it to start with, but resist adding more flour until it is fully developed. Once it has developed, you may need to dust down the bench lightly with a little flour when you come to scuffing up the dough or folding the dough through the bulk ferment process.

When fully developed and shaped into a nice tidy ball, all scuffed up and dusted down, then place it into the bowl with a little flour underneath and a little dusted on the top to help it fall away free from the bowl when you return to it. Cover with a plastic bag or lid to keep it supple and put to one side in the corner of the kitchen for 1 hour.

After 1 hour, lightly dust the work surface and bring the dough forward ready for the first fold. Tip it out of the bowl; it should fall freely from the bowl, avoiding unnecessary tearing of the dough. Once on the bench, take note of the amount of activity that has taken place. There will be very little at this stage, but that's all right, don't worry, we will now fold and stretch the little bit of cell structure in there to encourage the cells to multiply.

FOLDING THE DOUGH

You have this lump on the work surface looking at you; just press out deliberately, using the palm of the hands to form a rough rectangle, occasionally lifting it completely from the work bench to ensure it hasn't stuck. Dust a little more if necessary, then proceed to fold. This is done by bringing the bottom third over the middle third, stretching it a little as you go. Repeat this action by pulling the top third over the bottom and middle thirds, stretching a little as you do so. Rotate the whole of the dough piece 90 degrees. Using your fingertips, run all the way down from the top of the dough piece, pushing lightly on the way down to flatten and extend to the oblong shape required, then repeat the folding action as before. Once completed, turn over so the seam that you have created is now facing down. Place back into the lightly floured bowl and cover for the second bulk proof.

SECOND FOLD

After a further hour the dough is given a second fold. Before you repeat the folding, take note of the amount of gas that has now started to form. It will start to feel much lighter and more aerated. Tip it out on to the bench and repeat the action exactly as before, dust up and place seam side down back into a lightly floured bowl and cover it. This will then sit for just 30 minutes before processing.

PROCESSING

After 30 minutes, tip the dough out ready to scale to your required units. You will have a little over 1 kg of dough, so you could make one large loaf scaled off at 900g, finished bake weight 800g, and one 200g baton or 4 pittas, or it will make 2 x 450g small loaves plus the extras for 3 rolls, or just cut into 2 x 500g units, as weight accuracy will not be a factor in the domestic kitchen. Once you have scaled off your unit sizes, then lightly scuff (mould) up to form a uniform shape, but not as tight as for the products using brewer's yeast. If you like the random cell structure associated with the sourdough breads, place on a lightly floured work surface, and cover to avoid skinning. This will need just 15 to 20 minutes' intermediate proof to recover.

PREPPING BASKET

If you have a wicker basket, you will need to prepare it by sprinkling in a generous handful of flour and pushing it well into the grooves, so that the rim of each grove is just exposed, filling the grooves with excess flour ready for the moistures to penetrate through the final proof. Be careful not to tap it when you put it back down or the flour will fall back down to the bottom. If you use these regularly, resist the temptation to wash them, as this will make the wood moist and take a long time to dry out. Just brush them out well with a stiff brush after each use.

If you don't have a basket, then as suggested before, a bowl or plain bread basket with a well-floured tea towel will suffice, just something to support the dough through the final proof is all that is needed.

FINAL MOULD

For the final mould, the dough piece now needs to be moulded in a similar action to the folding carried out through each knock back. Lightly dust the bench, press out to a rectangle, fold over into three, rotate and repeat. Place into the basket with the seam facing up; this will ensure that when it is turned out to be set on to the hot tray or onto the sole of the oven, the seam will be at the base.

SETTING THE LOAF INTO THE OVEN

The oven is on and up to temperature, a hot tray is situated on a rack about a third of the way up in the oven, there is a hot pan with sides at the bottom of the oven, and half a cup of water is ready by the side. Tip the loaf out of the basket onto a lightly dusted slip (piece of thin ply or tray with no sides), make sure it is free running, then with a good sharp knife give one positive cut along the top, scoring quite deep to ensure the burst will take place. Open the oven door, set the loaf onto the hot tray, throw half a cup of cold water into the pan at the bottom, and close the door quickly to retain the steam to do its job.

The final bake will be about 25 to 30 minutes for an 800g loaf; from then on it is cosmetic as to how you like your breads to be.

SOURDOUGH OVERNIGHT

To extend the fermentation period for this bread will be no different from the breads set using brewer's yeast; the only thing to change will be the amount of yeast added. The above recipe will work just as well on a long ferment, but instead of adding 50% of the Mother as with the first dough, you will need to reduce this to just 20% of the flour weight. This amount will give you about 12 to 14 hours' bulk fermentation at an ambient temperature. This shows you how basic the yeast spores are; in the Mother it took just 0.5% of the brewer's yeast to flour weight to get the dough to perform in the same window. When the dough has been set, don't be tempted to prod it or knock it back at any time through the bulk proof; as demonstrated on the other dough, it will speed the process up, resulting in your having to reduce the final bulk time dramatically. You can also start to calculate how you can set a dough to perform in the window you want to work to by allocating more or less of the yeast to control it, or folding with a set amount of yeast to reduce the bulk time set (another new skill to practice and perfect).

The final stages using this dough will be no different from the first method given; it will just need the one knock back and intermediate proof before the final mould. The final proof will be about 1 hour; always bake under proved to get full benefit of the burst when it goes into the oven.

100% RYE BREAD

When I was an apprentice, this was one of the products I came to dread handling. It was one of the first jobs I would be given at some unearthly hour in the morning when I first walked through the door, much to the amusement of all the senior bakers, who would be offering their (what I know now to be impossible) suggestions on how to handle it. I would be presented with 280 lb of gloopy putty sitting in a massive mixing bowl, which was set at such a height that you knew it was going to be a back-breaking experience to process it. When I first started, there would be a couple of hours of continual ribbing by all, as this putty-like dough would slowly take me over, creeping up my arms and over my clothes, sticking me to everything I came into contact with. Through the day this would set like concrete on you, making you realise just how far something like this could travel, turning up in the strangest of places. On returning home exhausted after my day's work and falling asleep in the chair, I would be reprimanded for all the crunchy bits of dough that would fall off me onto the best chairs and floor.

One of the best suggestions by the lads was that the bowl would tip to a forty-five degree angle if the pin was removed. This was fine and would save the back, but what they didn't tell me was that once this bowl went past a certain angle, because of the weight of the dough inside, there was no return. Unfortunately the dough was at such a consistency that it just wanted to keep creeping forward, and there was no way I could scale off to keep up with this relentless mass creeping forward, and guess what, just when I needed help to lift the bowl back up, there was no one to be found; everyone had gone for a break. This was all part of the apprenticeship, and something you would have to ride with to gain the senior bakers' respect, hoping then they would pass on the all-important snippets of information they had.

The up side was this product would only be produced once or twice a week; the down side was you never knew which day the boss was going to put the production run on, so it was a continual surprise. Through practice, speed would eventually win through. Once this happened, it became a challenge to beat your previous time, making it more of a pleasure and giving a sense of achievement, when you realised you had mastered another skill in your chosen trade.

In the domestic kitchen, although you will only be making one or two loaves at a time, this will still happen with the first few you produce. You will possibly find it a little difficult and messy to handle, but with practice it will become much easier, helping this to become one of the breads you will want to add to your skills. There are many different ways to keep yourself free from the dough when handling it. To produce this range using the baskets or bowl with a cloth, I would recommend using flour to coat the dough piece, just as you did when handling the soda breads, as this will prevent it from sticking to anything, and also give it a lovely rustic appearance when baked. If you are making this dough into tin breads, then continually coating your hands and work surface with oil and/or water is helpful, but oil will encourage large holes throughout the finished loaf if care is not taken to ensure it is limited to just the outside surface of the loaf.

To produce these breads requires 100% rye Mother to 100% medium rye flour, so ensure you have sufficient Mother fully fed for the recipe size you have chosen to make. Also ensure that this has been fed at least 12 hours before you want to build the loaf, and that you will be left with a small amount of Mother after you have taken the recipe amount away, to keep ready for a big feed for the next production run, whenever that will be. It is always better to over feed from a small amount retained rather than under feed from a large amount retained. Don't forget the consistency you run the Mother at will also have a big influence on the dough, so discretion and skill will definitely need to be applied when setting this type of dough. The slacker you can set the rye doughs, without creating problems for yourself when handling, will be an advantage to help it to spring into action when exposed to the heat in the oven. Because Mother is being added at such high levels on such a short process, there will be little chance of complementing or stabilising it through the process, so the condition of the Mother will be paramount in determining the quality of the finished article, and great emphasis should be placed on caring for her prior to the production.

This loaf is produced without any bulk proof or intermediate proofs, just a final proof, so it is advisable to prepare your basket first, to save you having to stop to do this once you are all stuck up. A thin plastic scraper will be a useful piece of equipment to have by your side, as you will need to scrape down the bowl well. A generous handful of flour by your side on the work surface is recommended, so that you are ready when you come to coat the dough before adding to the basket or lined bowl. If you are producing both the soda and rye breads on a regular basis, it often helps to speed things up if you have a small amount of, say, a coarse dark rye flour ready in a large bowl; this then can be used each time for both of these breads, thus eliminating waste. You can then add a little fresh flour to this each time it is used; cover it when finished ready for the next time you want to call on it. If you are using a pile on the work bench, be generous with the amount, but don't waste it when you have finished, just sieve it out to add to the next run.

These breads are still produced in great numbers throughout many parts of Europe, with many different textures and base flavours. They are also complemented with the high addition of seeds, with subtle flavours of some spices to tease the palate. As far as I could work out, in certain parts of Germany caraway seeds are added at varying levels, depending on the region, or what they will be eating or drinking with these breads. This wonderful flavour had also been forgotten in this country, so it became an additional barrier to the acceptance of these breads when I was trying to promote them through the bad times.

When traveling through the south of France, I came across a village bakery making sour dough with a fantastic subtle after flavour that would linger with you on the palate for a long time. When I went in to work with the baker, mainly to see how he achieved this, I was surprised to find out it was just ground aniseed and toasted wheat bran. WOW! So simple. When I returned home, this was to become the birth of the rye bread recipe that follows. By just adding a few aniseeds and chopped dried figs to a forgotten bread, it complements a whole range of cheeses, especially the blue ones, and it has now proved to be one of the most popular breads. When a variety of breads are presented at lunch time at the workshops, it brings me great pleasure to see six people sitting around a table, tucking into the breads that were so easily rejected only thirty-five years earlier. As with so many breads, if they are produced correctly, they will carry almost any addition. A few suggestions for this one, other than the fig and aniseed, are walnut and raisin with a very small amount of caraway seed; dried apricots and toasted almonds with a hint of cinnamon; or just simply soak the whole rye grain overnight with equal amounts of water and a little of the Mother, just as they would traditionally do for the pumpernickel breads, then add this to the dough the next day. It gives that lovely chewy texture to the bite. You could add a few black onion seeds with this; they really sing well together; sunflower seed, pumpkin seed and sesame with a very few fresh herbs all complement dried meats and soft cheeses, and fennel is good as an add-on to the fish dishes.

Note: The salt added to this dough will be running at 3% of the flour weight. This is not a mistake; it is added to counterbalance the high addition of the rye Mother dough.

ANISE SEEDS

The actual anise seed is difficult to find in this country, but look in the health food shops. It is starting to appear there, or if you purchase the star anise and run the whole star through a coffee grinder, it will make it into a fine powder that will work just as well. It will also give the next run of coffee a lovely added flavour.

ONE HUNDRED PERCENT RYE BREAD		
INGREDIENTS	%	GRAMS
Medium rye flour	100	300
Salt	3	9
Rye Mother	100	300
Water	80	240
Dried diced figs	42	126
Anise seeds	0.5	1.5
	Total	976
Finished dough temperature 28°C		

METHOD

Place the flour, salt, Mother, anise seeds and tempered water into the bowl, then using your hand, start to bring it together. Once it has started to form a paste, scrape the bowl down and continue to beat until it forms a smooth soft putty appearance. Now fold in the dried figs gently, making sure the figs do not bleed out through the dough, but hold their diced shape. Scoop out as much of the dough from the bowl as you can and place gently on the pile of flour ready by your side, then return to the bowl to scrape down the residue. This then can be added to the sticky side of the larger portion of dough. Once it is all together, proceed to coat the whole of the outside of the dough with the flour. It will be a little tricky but something that will improve with practice. As soon as it is coated, place into the basket or lined bowl and just tap gently to hold the shape. Cover to give the final proof of 1 hour.

Note: If you are using a planetary mixer, then a beater will be more efficient in mixing this dough than the dough hook.

BAKING RYE BREADS

For the bake, I personally favour a darker well-baked crust, as you find them in many parts of Germany. This is created for the cosmetic appearance as well as for flavour, but the main reason is that traditionally they are not eaten until they are three or four or more days old. This gives them time to mature internally, and the thick hard crust will gradually soften as it is exposed to the atmosphere. It will also help to retain the moisture longer internally, giving the flavours longer to mingle. They don't expect their breads to be soft and pappy; they expect to chew for longer as part of the pleasure of eating. The more mature the loaf, the easier it will be to break down on the palate when chewing, so giving you the full advantage of the flavours within. Try cutting a slice off each day from day 1, day 2, day 3 and so on, and think about what goes on in your mouth and which day brings you most pleasure when chewing (you are in control).

Set the oven to the highest temperature you have in a domestic oven or about 300°C for an industrial oven. Once up to temperature, and just before you set the breads onto the hot surface you have created, or the sole of the oven, turn the temperature down to 230°C, prepare your slip as before and gently tip out the dough from the basket. Don't cut, just straightaway set the breads into the oven with a little steam, as created on the bake for the other breads. Close the door and give the bread about 1 hour's bake. In some European bakeries I have worked in, they even wind the oven temperature back up to 300°C for the final 10 minutes or so of the bake, to intensify this effect.

With certain 100% rye breads produced in Germany, they wash the surface of the loaf with scalded rye flour, just as we did for the skilly wash. This creates a blind surface without any rustic cracks, if you prefer a smooth surface.

SOFT ROLL AND BAP, TIN BREAD, LARDY CAKE

Concentrated fermentation will enhance crust retention, make functional glutens more fragile, thus aiding digestion, as well as adding flavour to make it how we want it to be. This product will help you to understand how you can aim for a softer eating texture produced on a short process, while still benefiting from sponges being added for flavour and digestion. Adding the flying sponge will also ensure the yeasts are multiplying well before introducing the full dough. The range we produce with it will best demonstrate its advantages as a soft dough, baps, tin bread and lardy cake. It can also be used to create soft dinner rolls, and a wholemeal version of this recipe can be used for the old English bobbins (explained in my favourite forgotten recipes later). This will work just as well as the one suggested that would have originally been used to produce them.

Extra equipment needed will be a fork to dock the tops of the baps, baking trays with baking parchment if not non-stick, a baking pan with sides for the lardy, a rolling pin, and a loaf tin measuring roughly 20 by 10cm (8 by 4 inches), or a little smaller if you can find it. The choice of bread tins for domestic use does seem to be very limited; they all seem too large for a small loaf and not large enough for a large loaf. If you can't find the one you want, then make a wooden frame and line it with baking parchment; this works just as well. The extra ingredients needed to produce the full range will be soft brown sugar, raisins, mixed spice, lard, soya flour, light rye, and malt extract. Both the soya and the malt extract can be found in health food shops, and don't forget the all-important overnight sponge or your pinch back sitting in the fridge.

By now this should be second nature to you if not practicing the pinch back system but I will put it down just in case.

OVERNIGHT SPONGE		
INGREDIENTS	%	GRAMS
Flour	100	100
Salt	2	2
Yeast	1	1
Water	60	60

Mix to a silky dough and leave covered in the kitchen overnight for at least 12 to 14 hours.

MAIN DOUGH RECIPE		
INGREDIENTS	%	GRAMS
Flour, white	100	500
Overnight sponge or pinch back	30	150
Salt	2	10
Yeast	2.5	12.5
Lard	2	10
Soya flour	2	10
Light rye flour	2	10
Malt extract	1	5
Water	70	350
	Total	1057

The finished dough temperature should be 25°C, but do the calculations on 30°C, as the flying sponge will sit around for 40 minutes losing heat, and the overnight sponge or pinch back may well be cool.

METHOD

Weigh 100g of flour into a bowl large enough for the batter when it doubles in size, add the yeast and just 150g of the total water allocated for the full recipe. Beat this to a creamy batter and put to one side until it drops.

While this is taking place, weigh the remaining ingredients, including the remaining water, into a larger bowl, but remember you have already taken 100g from the total flour weight, so you will only be weighing in the remaining 400g necessary to bring it to the 500g allocated for the full recipe when both parts are brought together. You will also have only 200g of water remaining to be added, for the same reason. All the ingredients go into the bowl, with exception of the lard and the sponge. This is placed on the work surface to be added half way through the dough development, just as we did with the butter in enriched dough and the sponge on the very first dough to produce the cottage breads, both for the same reasons as explained in each recipe method.

When the sponge has dropped, add this to the remaining ingredients in the larger bowl, and continue to hydrate. Once this has taken place, then out on the work top it comes to develop to the full dough. It will be slack, but should still clear both the bench and your hands when fully developed. When it is nice and silky, dust up to form a tidy ball, and place back into the bowl, cover and put to one side for the bulk fermentation.

Everything we have done to this product has been to eliminate crust, so to complement this process, the bulk proof will be limited to just 30 minutes. After this time it will be ready to start processing, with just one short intermediate proof. The range of products given will best demonstrate the advantages of this dough, but don't confine yourself to this range. This dough can be used for any product you want, if you need it to be soft in texture and crust with a fine close crumb structure. (You are now moving close to becoming a baker, so you decide, not the recipe book.) The dough will be slack, so may well benefit from a little dusting of flour on the work surface through all of the procedures, but not in excess, as this will make it difficult when moulding to form the required shapes.

SCALE OFF

4 x 80g for the baps.
1 x 200g for the lardy cake.
The remaining 500g plus will be for the small tin loaf.

Once weighed, scuff up the 4 x 80g units and the 200g unit and place on a well-floured work bench. The largest piece will also need to be scuffed to form a neat shape, but placed on just a little flour. Cover them all for just 15 minutes of intermediate proof.

While this is happening, prep your baking tray. Either lightly grease or cover with baking parchment. Also prepare the small baking pan with baking parchment and sprinkle a little sugar in the base to place the lardy on when ready. Next, either line your wooden frame with baking parchment or grease the bread tin, ready for the 500g tin loaf.

BAPS

Bring forward the 4 x 80g units and make sure they are well floured both sides, then using the rolling pin, roll out each one to a 10cm (4 inch) circle, continually coating with flour to prevent them from sticking to the work top. When all 4 are completed, place on the baking tray and dock (stab) well with the fork, making sure you have covered all the surface with small pin holes. This will prevent them from popping when baked, eliminating any chance of them forming a hollow just under the surface. Cover with plastic and prove for 40 minutes before baking in an oven pre-heated to 230°C. The bake will be about 10 to 12 minutes, and they should be taken out before they take any crust colour, if you want them to be soft to the bite when cool. If unsure whether they are done, use your thermometer to probe the core and as soon as it reaches 94°C to 96°C take them out.

TIN BREAD

When you come to the small loaf moulding, you could decide just to process into one unit, moulding as tight as you can without tearing the outer surface. To create a finer crumb, you could practise cross panning to encourage the cell structure to be sideways on when the finished loaf is sliced, rather than being a cell that you can look through if you don't cross pan. This is difficult to explain but easy to demonstrate. You have a cell, so when moulding, if you only roll this out to form a sausage, then that cell will just be elongated, forming a tube when baked. See the illustration below. Each slice of the loaf will look through the cell, creating a darker coarse-looking crumb structure.

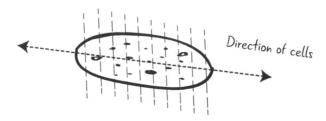

You can either cut that elongated dough piece into four pieces and place them into the tin sideways on, the cells will then be going from side to side rather than through from end to end, creating the image of a whiter softer crumb. Or you could mould up four equal-sized units into a nice tight round shape and put them into the tin, which will do the same job of confusing the cell structure.

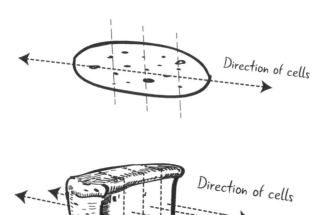

Bring forward the 500g unit, and if you decide to cross pan, mould to a nice tight ball, then roll out to elongate it to about 30cm (12 inches). You may need to let it rest for a little while to achieve this. Cut into 4 equal-sized pieces and then lay them in the bread tin sideways on. If you chose to make it into one single piece, then mould to a nice tight round shape and then elongate to fit your tin size. Cover with plastic, and the final proof on this loaf will be about 30 to 35 minutes, but it is advisable to bake under-proved rather than over-proved. It will need to go in the oven with plenty of tension under the surface, so when you gently prod the surface with a finger, it should still bounce back. If it leaves an indentation, you know you have stepped over the line and you will need to set it a little earlier next time. Normally these breads are dusted lightly on the surface with a little flour just before baking to prevent the steam from gelatinising the surface starches. When this is added, it will help them to stay soft.

They will benefit from a little steam being added to the chamber to encourage them to stay supple through the early stages of the bake, helping with even oven spring. This steam will need to be pulled out by opening the door of the oven to extract it after the first 5 minutes into the bake. This will eliminate any chance of it creating crust retention through the bake. Cut the surface of the loaf to encourage it to spring where you want it to spring when it kicks into life in the oven, and set onto a hot baking surface, as with all the other breads we have made. Bake in a pre-heated oven set at 230°C for about 25 minutes minimum for a soft eating crust. Once baked, tap out of the tin as soon as it is manageable, to prevent it from sweating in the tin.

LARDY CAKE

Once again, there are many different versions of this product. The Wiltshire lardy is rolled up in the shape of a very large Chelsea bun, cut up and baked in a pan, swirl side up. This is all right if you are making a lot of them but it's difficult to do if you are producing just the one. The one we are making for demonstration purposes seems to be christened the Dorset lardy, but when I was working as an apprentice, we made them in a very similar process, just slightly fatter in depth; they had no regional identification.

LARDY CAKE FILLING		
INGREDIENTS	%	GRAMS
Lexia raisins	100	100
Soft brown sugar	60	60
Lard	30	30
Mixed peel	25	25
Mixed spice	2	2
	Total	217

Blend the lard, sugar and spice together to make a paste, and then add the raisins and mixed peel to make a nice tight ball. Put this to one side ready to use later. If you can prepare it the night before there are benefits but it's not important. A lot of people don't like the mixed candied peel, so this can be replaced with fresh orange and lemon zest if need be.

METHOD

Bring forward the lardy cake filling made before the process started. You should also have 1 x 200g unit left to process. It is now well proved and relaxed. Handle it without knocking it back too much, as this will make it easier to roll out. Make sure it is well coated with flour, and that there is always a little flour on the bench to prevent it from sticking, then with the rolling pin, roll out to form a rectangle reaching 25cm long by 15cm wide (10 by 6 inches). Make sure it is free from the bench before starting to spread the lardy filling over two-thirds of the surface of the shaped dough.

The next stage is called lamination, a process which is like what you would do when creating a puff pastry or croissant or Danish pastry. Each stage when completed is called a half turn, 2 half turns will be equal to 1 full turn. The puff has 6 half turns or 3 full turns, a croissant and Danish will only receive 3 half turns or in some cases 1 half turn and 1 book turn. A book turn equates to 1 1/4 half turns, creating a lighter eating product if you wish (you are in control). I don't tell you all this to confuse you, it will hopefully ring bells when you come to working with laminated products. The humble lardy only requires 2 half turns.

Once you have rolled out the dough, spread the filling over the two-thirds; bring the third without any filling on up to cover the middle third with the filling on. Repeat the process with the remaining third that has the filling on, forming a layer of dough, layer of filling, layer of dough, layer of filling, layer of dough. Rotate the whole of the dough

90 degrees, ensuring it is well floured and free from the bench, ready to pin out to the original shape you rolled the dough out to, 25cm by 10cm or thereabouts is fine. When pinning out, it is advisable to bring it down to the required dimensions gradually, to avoid tearing the outside surface or squeezing too much of the filling out as you do so. Give 1 half turn, bottom third over the middle third, top third over the middle third, rotate 90 degrees, ensuring it is well floured, and repeat this to create another half turn, equalling 1 full turn. Once completed, pin out to your required size to place in the pan on top of the sprinkled sugar. In some parts of Dorset, they were traditionally pinned down to about 20cm (8 inches). The final proof will be about 30 minutes, and the bake time will be dependent on the thickness you have chosen to make them to. Although they are classed as a sweet product, I would still prefer to bake these at 220°C to 230°C on a hot surface in the oven. Baking this way, all of the sugar will caramelise very quickly. As soon as this starts to happen, it is a good indication that it is baked. About 12 to 15 minutes is a good guide, and a light bake is recommended. Once baked and out of the oven, just give it a few minutes to rest, then turn out while still warm, taking care not to burn yourself, as hot sugar will stick to you and can be painful.

OPEN CRUMB

To produce this range of breads, it will be necessary to work with overnight saltless sponges. They will demand high hydration at both the sponge and the dough stage, helping to push your skills a little further forward when setting and handling this dough, which is one of the reasons I have chosen to add it to the range. It is typically used for the production of Ciabatta and Focaccia, as this recipe will be. The French also use many different versions based around this method. They work with much lower additions of yeast and cooler doughs, to compensate for the lower proteins in the flour they use, as for many years they have been encouraged to work only with the grain grown in France. Wheat grown in this country is no different; they have similar proteins, so when working with these flours, some bakers choose to retard the sponges or reduce the yeast levels if running at ambient, to help them tolerate the long ferments. The water absorption at the second stage is not added, and then they would prove the finished article at about 12°C for 12 to 18 hours. No wonder this craft is disappearing as their pace of life increases. It could take up to 30 hours to produce an authentic French baguette. That's how they obtained those lovely crusts you would normally have found in many bakers in France if you went back just twenty years ago. There is also reference to this method in my Grandad's notes when he was working on product development to produce open crumb Vienna breads for the Lyons tea shops. I'm not sure of the date but assume it would be the 1930s or 1940s. This is one of the many questions I wish I had asked him; I'm sure he had most of the answers, and could have saved me the time of re-inventing the wheel on many occasions.

A fascinating story I heard when baking with a few bakers in northern Italy was that the breads such as the slipper breads and Focaccia and possibly the Pizza came about relatively recently. As far as I can make out, with my poor understanding of the Italian language, and the few words of English the bakers had, and many pictures drawn in the flour dust on the work bench, not forgetting the large amounts of local wine drunk through the night's work, I may well have some of the information wrong but the story has it that a father went away and left his young son to make the breads while he was away. He made a mistake when setting the overnight doughs and forgot to put the salt in, an easy mistake to make and it can happen to any of us (I'm talking from experience). He soon realised his mistake in the morning, when he arrived to find the dough had over-fermented and spewed all over the bakery. In his panic, his answer was to scoop it all up, place it back into the mixing bowl, add the salt and more flour to try to compensate for the over-fermentation, more yeast to help it to kick in again, and more water to get it to the right consistency. For all his efforts, the dough became very slack and tacky when being developed, because of the over-fermentation, so he kept mixing in the hopes he could salvage his mistake. Eventually it cleared, but the dough was now moving like a train, so as soon as he scaled the units off, he baked them by setting them onto the sole of the oven to stop them from flowing. This was the birth of the slipper bread (maybe).

After he had scaled off his numbers required, he had another problem. There was this mass of dough left over, so the next day he had a repeat of the same method, to try to hide his mistake before his father returned. Luckily for him, it was to become a success, and soon became a method throughout his product range, and many other bakers throughout the region copied it. I'm not sure of the authenticity of this story, but it helped me to understand the method used in their breads, and having had many disasters when pushing the boundaries of product development, it is a story I can relate to. As with all breads, they evolve. With the renewed interest we now have in this country in real breads, it is the perfect opportunity for the next generation of up-and-coming bakers to carry this momentum forward, just as this young lad did, with or without intention. We have the potential of gaining world recognition for our breads; as our quality improves, other European countries are on the decline. They are only thirty years behind in discovering the consequences of speed in their foods.

The sponges will need at least 12 to 14 hours to ferment, so you need to plan ahead. The final stages of the process will be relatively quick, about 1½ hours from the start of the second stage of the process, and your breads will be out of the oven.

OVERNIGHT SPONGE FIRST STAGE		
INGREDIENTS	%	GRAMS
White flour	100	300
Yeast, fresh*	6	6
Cold water	100	300
	Total	606

*Mother yeast can be used at this stage of the dough and will bring a more authentic flavour to the bread, but it will need to be increased from 2% to 10% of the flour weight.

Mother can also be used in the final stage but it needs be increased to 15% of the flour weight on the second stage and will also need to have 2 hours' bulk fermentation with 3 folds within this time period to achieve the same effect as the fresh yeast.

METHOD

Place the ingredients in a bowl large enough to allow for the expansion through the fermentation, and large enough to be able to beat in the other ingredients on the second stage the morning. About a 4 to 5 litre capacity bowl is a good guide.

By hand, beat to a thick creamy batter, making sure all the lumps are dispersed. Cover and set to one side in the kitchen for 12 to 14 hours.

MAIN DOUGH SECOND STAGE		
INGREDIENTS	%	GRAMS
Flour	100	150
Salt	6	9
Fresh yeast	6	9
Overnight sponge	400	600
Water*	67	100**
	Total	868

This dough needs to be set at the magic 28°C and the calculations still need to be made. I would advise you to use the temperature of the overnight sponge to calculate this figure, as it is added at such a high percentage.

IMPORTANT NOTES

*Adding the water to the second stage of this dough is critical, and the only tricky part of building this dough. After the dough has been developed, the water needs to be added a little at a time, say in 5 or 6 portions, and cleared after each addition. It can be difficult to achieve if making by hand, and there is lots of arm ache, but it is necessary if you want to get the water fully incorporated. If you are using a small planetary mixer at home, then I would recommend using the beater rather than the dough hook. You only have a very small amount of fresh flour going in on the second stage, so adding the moistures to this slowly will give them a chance to hydrate, open up and swell before the next addition. Also the concentrated acidities within the first part of the dough will be encouraging this to happen, but need time to do their job. If you add all the water in one go, it will flow and never regain the structure needed to create these breads. When completed, the dough will definitely be very slack but manageable, and, with time, will clear the bowl when picked up. If not, it will only be down to the fact that the moistures have been added too quickly. If you are concerned that it may be difficult for you to achieve this on your first couple of goes, then it may be better to leave some of the water out so you are comfortable handling it, then push your skills a little further by adding more of the water content recommended each time you make it this. Precaution may avoid disappointment.

If using this dough for Focaccia, I was taught to add the olive oil liberally on the outside just before the bake, so if this is your choice, you will need olive oil, fresh or dried herbs and sea salt crystals ready for the top finish just before they are set into the oven. If using this dough for Ciabatta, then incorporate olive oil equivalent to 10% of flour weight added into the dough in the second stage after the second hydration has taken place. Adding oils to these doughs too early will have the same effect as the butter and fats in an enriched dough or a pastry, coating the flour particles, so isolating them from the moisture, and with these hydration levels, the dough will definitely become unmanageable.

This method is used to produce French breads; the only difference is that it is produced using their own low protein French flour, there is no second addition of water and in some bakeries they retard the overnight sponge, and possibly also the final proof may be retarded, depending on their beliefs and their desire to create an authentic loaf.

A true pizza dough will be made using exactly the same sponge. There are definitely advantages to setting this sponge using the rye Mother as your yeast source on the first stage. They normally use a higher protein flour; once again there is no water addition to the second stage. These recipes will be given later under the heading of **Recipes regularly requested** but it is the right opportunity now for me to explain that there is little mystery to a whole range of breads; once you start to work with them regularly, you realise how simple it can be, helping you to do quick calculations to achieve the desired results. This will be no different when you work with your favourite recipe book at home. This knowledge will help you achieve the right texture and taste, just like the bread in the glossy picture (your knowledge now puts you in control).

These doughs need little final proof, so make sure the oven is on in advance, also that your thick baking tray is in there ready, as these breads will need to be baked on a solid hot surface to get the best oven spring from them. This will help to open up the crumb. The temperature is set to 230°C ready to go when needed.

You could even decide to add this sponge to the very first dough set down in the basic dough section, to make the cottage range. It will work just as well, the taste will be different and the crumb cell structure will be more open. This may be something you favour; have a go and christen it with your own name so it's your creation rather than follow my leader.

METHOD

Bring forward the overnight ferment, add the flour, salt, and fresh yeast, then mix this to a dough. It can be achieved in the bowl, but some find it more comfortable to scoop it out onto the work surface to complete the development. It will be slack and tacky but don't be tempted to add more flour. Be persistent and continue to tear and stretch, pulling the heel of your hand through, having a scrape up every now and then to keep it tidy. It will eventually clear the bench when picked up. Once this has happened, add just a little of the water and continue until clear, add and clear, in 5 or 6 additions. Some find this part of the process easier to add in the bowl, as it is difficult to get off of your shoes and the kitchen floor if it goes horribly wrong. If you do get tired, rest for a few minutes, then add more water and continue to develop. It won't do it any harm to have a rest. Once all the liquid has been added, scrape down the bowl and put to one side for about 15 minutes to allow it to relax before giving it another good thrashing. If making a Ciabatta, this would be the time to beat in the olive oil. Once completed, scrape down once again, then gently trickle olive oil all the way around the edge, running it down the inside of the bowl until you get back to where you started. Using your fingers, slowly slide them down the side until you reach the bottom, allowing the olive oil to flow underneath each time you do this on your way around the bowl. Eventually the dough will become free from the bowl and flow freely, suspended in a little olive oil. Cover and put to one side for 30 minutes if using fresh yeast.

Bring forward to give just one knock back. This will need to be done in the bowl by stretching the dough over itself just a few times; no need to be too thorough with the process. This will help to create a more random open cell structure. It should still be spinning freely in the bowl, suspended in the excess olive oil.

PROCESSING

Twenty minutes after the knock back, you can start to process the dough. Bring it forward, make sure it is still flowing free from the bowl, and evenly dust the work surface with a good handful and a bit of flour. Spread this evenly using your fingertips, making sure it covers an area about 35cm (14 inches) square. Now be brave, pick up the bowl and up-end it in one action. Hopefully it will fall neatly on to the flour that you have spread onto the work surface if you have been lucky. As soon as it is on the floured bench, pull and stretch the bottom edge to the centre, then pull and stretch the left hand side edge over to the centre, followed by the top edge and right edge, making sure it is well dusted at all times. This should now have formed a nice tidy square with a fluffy pillow-like feel to the touch when prodded. There are advantages to turning the whole dough piece over so that all the seams are underneath but this is not essential. Try it when you are feeling confident and no one is looking.

If using for Ciabatta, stretch it one way a little to extend it to about 45cm by 30cm (18 by 12 inches), then, using a scraper, chop off into 4 equal-sized pieces with a rough dimension of 30cm by 10cm (12 by 4 inches), making sure they are well coated with flour to keep free from you, the bench, and each other.

They will only need about 15 minutes' final proof, and they will be less likely to flow if this proof is carried out on a tea towel that has been heavily dusted with a coarse product such as ground rice or semolina. Once proved, these will need to be slipped straight on to the hot sole created in the oven, with a little steam. The bake will be light; this should be achieved within 8 to 10 minutes.

If Focaccia is your choice, then treat the dough exactly the same when preparing the product on the bench. After this you could decide to just make one large one, or divide it to make two smaller ones. After the proving time, these products will normally be baked on the sole of the oven just as with the Ciabatta, but as the oil is being added on the outside of the product, there is a tendency for the oil to spill over when being baked, creating many unwanted problems in a domestic oven. It would be advisable to bake them in a baking pan with sides to prevent this happening. For two Focaccia made from this volume of dough, I normally use the same pan size as used for the Chelsea buns. Once you have prepared your pan or pans by lining with baking parchment, place the dough piece or pieces into them, gently but firmly press out using the finger tips to fill the pan and set to one side for 10 minutes.

PREPPING FOR OVEN

Have your bottle of olive oil, fresh or dried herbs, and the salt crystals ready close by. Bring the dough forward and lightly coat the top surface with a little olive oil. Once again using your fingertips, probe all the way through to the base in a dense pattern, working your way down from the top to the bottom. Now trickle olive oil liberally all over the surface. This oil should then fill the indentations made with the fingers. When baked, this olive oil should become trapped inside, so when sliced cold, the oil should flow out, adding to the authentic experience of this bread. Sprinkle lightly with herbs and salt crystals, then put it straight into the oven. If baked on the sole of the oven, the bake time should be very similar to the Ciabatta, but in a pan, just allow a few more minutes to compensate for the thickness of the pan.

SCONES

This product is in between a soda bread and a pastry, and the reason it is included in the advanced course is purely to demonstrate the importance of using your ingredients to your advantage, so if you love the scones you make, please don't change them. I have learnt that some people can be very protective and defensive of their scones, but if you want to improve on yours, just adopt some of the logic that follows, and it may well help. It will be aerated using the same principle of activating bicarbonate of soda with the acidity in buttermilk, and not using baking powder or self-raising flour, as these have an undesirable after taste. The only magic ingredient in this product that can change the eating quality of the finished article is the butter. As with the pastry on the basic course, it is used to achieve the shortest possible bite in anything using flour, fat and water. In this product we only have 20% fat being added, so this small amount will need to be rubbed around as many particles of flour as possible, protecting them from the added moistures. This prevents them from becoming elastic, and creates a shorter bite when eaten.

If you are making something like rock cakes or raspberry buns (one of the first things I made at college) the fats will be much lower and the liquids will be higher. Because of this, more particles will be exposed and so will gelatines, resulting in the bite on this product being harder and more crumbly. A scone should not eat like this. Historically the true Cornish scone would have had a small amount of nutmeg added. As with the saffron buns, as the spices started to filter through the Plymouth docks, they would be the first to add them to their products to give them regional identity, like the Irish country folk. I'm sure the buttermilk would have been used after they had extracted the butter; I can't accept that this would have been wasted, as country folk would have needed to be very careful with their resources.

As with the soda breads, this product will have a limited time after it has been mixed before it starts to gas itself out, so make sure the oven is up and running at 200°C before you start.

SCONE RECIPE

INGREDIENTS	%	GRAMS
White flour	100	400
Salt	1	4
Fine sugar	20	80
Butter	20	80
Bicarbonate of soda	1.5	6
Nutmeg to taste		
Buttermilk	60	240
	Total	810

METHOD

Blend the buttermilk and sugar together in a jug. If you can do this the night before and keep it in the fridge, it will give the two ingredients time to emulsify fully, reducing the chance of sugar spots appearing on the surface of the scone when baked. Place all the remaining ingredients into a large bowl and proceed to rub the fat into the flour, salt and bicarb. Once it has begun to form a crumb, start to rub it through the palms of your hands, pushing them against each other, working them in a circular motion with the mixture in between, and replenishing each time you dive back in. When you think you have rubbed enough, rub some more. This is the point that will make the difference between a soft-eating scone and a hard rock cake texture when eating. When you are happy with the consistency, add the buttermilk and sugar, blend them in, then bring together to form a dough. When this has happened, tip it out onto the work surface and continue to develop to a smooth dough. Have no fear of it toughening up. If you want to add fruit, this would normally be sultanas, added at 35% to 40% of the flour weight. Because of the way this product has been produced, you can mix them in after it has formed a dough.

Dust down the bench and roll out the dough to your preferred thickness. Cut out your shapes, gather up your remaining scraps, and once again there is little need to respect this when mixing back together, as there will be little toughening taking place before you cut out the remainder. When baking scones, it is advisable to place them on a baking sheet so that they are not quite touching. This helps them to grow evenly through the bake. It will also help to keep the sides from colouring up too much, keeping them soft and fleshy to the bite when eaten. We want the surface to stay soft, so they will be washed with protein, such as egg or milk; egg will give a better glaze. Bake in a pre-set oven at 200°C for 12 minutes. A light bake is recommended.

A scone round would often be made at the bakery, especially at weekends. It would be the same mix but without fruit, weighed off into 250g units, roughly shaped to a round, then pinned out to about 15cm, or in those days 6 inches. The top would be washed with milk and then dipped into sugar nibs.

If you want to make cheese scones, remove the sugar from the recipe above and add grated strong cheese and pepper or mustard powder. I have seen paprika used as well. The smaller ingredients are down to your discretion and personal taste, but the cheese volume is a little more difficult, as to get the full flavour into a cheese scone, the volumes of cheese necessary to get the right taste will start to affect the volume when baked. This can be overcome by using 25% of the flour weight in grated strong cheese, then add to this just 5% of the flour weight in finely grated hard cheese such as Parmesan.

Bread makers or bread machines

I have been in the privileged position of working with so many people around the work bench. As we go around the table at the start, introducing ourselves, I ask them about their bread-making skills. This helps me to find out how much they know, and also helps me to make the day comfortable for all of us. Some seem almost embarrassed to admit that they are using a bread machine to produce their breads, as if I would think less of them for it, but it is to the contrary. Many people over the years have found inspiration from starting out using them, and those who become fascinated by the process can't seem to resist taking the dough out to play with after it has developed. The thing I personally dislike with them is the suggested recipes in the books they provide. They do seem very fond of adding fats, sugars and milk powders, and bundle them all in together at the start of the process. These are ingredients I prefer to use for the enriched breads rather than all breads, and I can't see the logic in adding them, other than softening the protein strands, making it easier for the little paddle in the machine to develop the dough.

The same logic applies to a bread maker as with any bread produce; adding fermentation to the dough will complement the process, rather than adding the wrong ingredients at the wrong time. All the methods practiced in the afore-mentioned doughs will work just as well when set in a bread maker using a basic setting; you just need to work ahead.

The fast-acting dried yeasts are designed for just this process, so if you don't have a problem with digesting these enhancers, add to them to your dough, but remember they work better on the shorter programme. If you choose to practise long fermentation in the form of setting overnight sponges or flying sponges, then these yeasts can work against you, as they become depleted very quickly, so the traditional yeasts are better to use.

If you have a Mother dough running, or even sitting idle in the fridge, then the obvious starting point will be to just add 10% of this to the normal dough you set in the bread maker, then run it on a basic programme. This will work as a natural enhancer, building stability into the dough through the process.

The next option is to set a small flying sponge, just as explained for the enriched dough. All you need to do is remember to start the process 45 minutes before you start the machine. This then can be added as soon as it drops. The flying sponge will allow you to use the yeasts without the flour treatment agents being added.

If you are using the bread maker to produce doughs with high fats or oils added, the same logic will need to be applied to this process as you would with any other dough. Keep them out until the moistures have just hydrated, then add the fats or oils. This will ensure that the moistures are within the flour particles before the fats or oils can coat them.

Bread makers are designed to simplify the process so any one can make bread, but more continuity can be obtained when some (if not all) the basic laws of fermentation are applied.

WE CAN ALL LEARN FROM YOUNG MINDS

My Granddaughter has invented this method through wanting to make bread with the knowledge and beliefs passed on by Granddad, but it also had to fit in with a busy twelve-year old's schedule. Bread machines had to be the answer.

On a Saturday she sets 500g of white flour, 10g of salt, 10g of fresh yeast and 300g of water into the bread maker, which is then set on just a mix program. Once it has completed, she removes it from the mixer, and places it into a bowl to ferment for a couple of hours.

Once fermented, it is divided into five equal pieces. One of the pieces is placed into the fridge, covered to avoid skinning; the remaining four pieces are placed into the freezer. (I'm not sure of the logic of this as it would be perfectly all right sitting in the fridge for the time she chooses to use it in, but it is her recipe and I'm proud that she has taken the time and trouble to work this out in her own mind.) On a Monday, before she rushes off for school, she sets the dough using just 400g of white flour, 8g of salt, 8g of fresh yeast and 250g of water, then starts the mixing on a basic program. She allows this to mix for a few minutes before lifting the lid to drop in the one piece of dough from the fridge, drops the lid and lets it complete the programme on its own. Just before she sets off for school she takes out one of the pieces of dough from the freezer and places it into the fridge; this will then be thawed enough to repeat the process by the next morning. The breads I have seen produced this way look and taste very good; her method is worth trying. I'm sure she will find a way of squeezing some royalty out of me for this information.

Recipes Regularly Requested

SPELT BREADS

The popularity of Spelt flour has increased dramatically since I was first introduced to it some twenty years ago. Obviously the grain has always been available, but I assume it fell from favour as we were led down the path of mass-produced high-volume bread.

Over the years it has proven to me to be a very unpredictable flour, despite the controls implemented by the miller. Every harvest has a wider range of variation than standard wheat, especially if it is in its organic form, so the new crop always brought new challenges.

It was an interesting learning curve for me, as this market opened up a new avenue of process and controls needed to ensure the best could be obtained from these delicate softer flours. A lot of people are now eating these breads, as they have gained the reputation of being better to digest for anyone with a gluten intolerance. They do still contain gluten, be it of a different make up. These glutens still need to be fermented, making sure they are broken down before you digest them, if you are to gain the full benefit from eating them. Making a spelt loaf using spelt flour on the Chorleywood method will provide very little benefit to your diet, other than the lovely sweet nutty flavours the flour will bring to the loaf.

When you start to add fermentation to these flours, because of their make-up, the window for optimum fermentation will start to close down. To enhance this fact, your doughs need to be set at a lower temperature, much as the French and all UK flours warrant. As the base of the flour is softer, the starch damage will be greater, exposing more of the natural maltose sugars. This will encourage the dough to move quicker, so lower yeast levels will need to be used, as well as lower temperature to help control it. Development time will need to be reduced when mixing the doughs, as the strands can quickly break down if put under too much pressure. Slower mixing will help to hold hydration; if mixed for too long and too quickly, moisture will be released, creating a tacky dough. This will not only make it difficult to handle; it will also have a detrimental effect on the finished crumb when the finished baked loaf ages.

Water absorption will fluctuate from bake to bake, so will need to be observed closely with each new bag of flour. Unfortunately this is the nature of the beast, and your skills will need to be applied to ensure consistency. The water absorptions will average some 2% to 3% lower than conventional flours. The doughs will benefit from being made much slacker in consistency than conventional doughs, as the doughs made with this flour seems to take the moistures on more slowly through the process. Slack is not to be confused with tacky to the touch through over-development.

I found the white and the wholemeal doughs needed to be set using totally different methods, just to confuse things even more with this flour. The wholemeal breads love short process, so to get some fermentation into this bread, I would set a slack overnight sponge using 20% of the flour and a little over equal amounts of water, adding just one third of your yeast allocation for the whole recipe. If you have a rye mother running, just adding 10% of flour weight used for this part of the dough in rye Mother works well, instead of the brewer's yeast.

The white flours seem to work best from the other end of the spectrum, using all the flour to make the dough, with 1% of the flour weight in brewer's yeast added or 15% of the rye Mother if preferred.

I always use the rye Mother with this flour, as its gluten content is very low. There would be little point in adding the high glutens in the white Mother made with conventional flour, as most people will have found their way to this particular flour through an intolerance to gluten. If producing this bread regularly because of an intolerance, then it is obviously worth the trouble of starting up a spelt Mother, using the white spelt rather than the wholemeal. I have found the wholemeal to have a rather bitter after-taste, even if the pH has been controlled. This taste is similar to a Mother made with barley flour, although not so prominent. If you have chosen to set the first stages of the wholemeal dough using any form of Mother, then the fresh yeast added on the second stage will be the only yeast required.

SUGGESTED WHOLEMEAL SPELT RECIPE

INGREDIENTS	%	GRAMS
Wholemeal spelt	100	500
Salt	2	10
Fresh yeast	3	15
Water	66	330
Oil or fat	1	5
	Total	860

FIRST STAGE SET 12 HOURS BEFORE NEEDED

INGREDIENTS	GRAMS
Wholemeal spelt	100
Cold water	110
Fresh yeast	5
Total	215

Beat this to a smooth batter and cover to avoid skinning, place in the corner of the kitchen for at least 12 hours running at an ambient temperature.

MAIN RECIPE FOR WHOLEMEAL SPELT

INGREDIENTS	GRAMS
Wholemeal spelt	400
Salt	10
Yeast	10
Oil or fat	5
Overnight sponge	215
Water	220
Total	860

Finished dough temperature 22°C to 25°C.
Bake temperature 220°C to 230°C.

In most good domestic ovens, the loaf will be baked well within the first 25 minutes; from then it will be cosmetic as to how you like your crust and colour.

METHOD

Place flour, salt and yeast into the bowl, making sure the yeast is away from the salt; add the overnight sponge, also water tempered to the correct degree to bring the dough to the required finished dough temperature.

Develop to full dough; it will slacken off dramatically through the development process, but will regain its correct structure as it passes through bulk proof. About three-quarters of the way through development, add the oil or fat. This addition may not be necessary with some harvests, but it is worth adding as a precaution, as on a poor year, the flour can lack its own natural fats normally found within the flour. This can cause a very fragile crumb in the finished loaf if not spotted.

Place into a bowl and cover, set to one side for just 30 minutes' bulk proof.

After the allocated time, bring forward and fold just the once (as described for the sour doughs), cover and rest for 15 minutes before scaling to your required weights.

Hand up to create a well-formed ball, and rest for just 10 minutes to recover, ready for the final mould to the shape of your preference.

The final proof is relatively short; make sure your oven is up to temperature well in advance, as there is a danger of over proof if left too long.

If you are working with oven bottom breads, then the final proof will only be 18 to 20 minutes from the final mould. If you are working with a tin, then 30 minutes is the longest you should leave it. Don't be tempted to prove longer, as the cell structure will become fragile very quickly, causing it to collapse when the heat hits it. It is always better to rely on the pent-up energy you have created to give the spring and volume, rather than expanding the cells to their full potential before baking. There is a danger with this flour of not being able to retain the last bit of gas given off, resulting in disappointment for you.

SPELT WHITE BREAD		
INGREDIENTS	%	GRAMS
White spelt flour	100	500
Salt	2	10
Fresh yeast	1	5
Water	57	285
Oil or fat	1	5
	Total	805

METHOD

Place the flour, salt, yeast and water into the mixing bowl, bring to dough, continue to develop until the dough is just starting to clear, add the fat or oil and continue to develop until it forms clear silky dough.

If you are using fresh yeast, then I would set the dough to one side (covered) at room temperature for 1 hour before retarding for 12 hours in a fridge or retarder running at between 6°C to 10°C, once again covered. If you are using the Mother dough as the yeast source, then I would set this to one side (covered) at room temperature for 2 hours. After this time has lapsed, then give the complete dough just one fold, as we did for the previous doughs when set using the Mother dough. Cover once again, then set this again into the retarder or domestic fridge for at least 12 hours.

When the allocated time has passed, it will need to be removed from its resting place. There will be a little activity that has taken place but not too noticeable, as most of the activity will have taken place internally. Scale into your required unit weights, and hand up to reintroduce the dormant yeast cells to fresh food. These will then quickly start to reactivate as the dough temperature starts to increase. Once handed up, set to one side, covered to avoid the surface forming a skin, and allow at least 30 minutes for the dough to recover.

The dough will now have started to move relatively quickly; all that is needed is to give the final tight mould to your required shape in either a tin or free standing.

Final proof will depend a lot on the ambient temperature in your working environment, as well as your choice of yeast used, so these times are just suggestions. It's well worth reiterating: never be tempted to push the cell structure to double its size, as suggested by so many domestic recipes. Always make sure you have plenty of energy in reserve in each cell. Use and improve your skills each time; you're in control.

For the loaf using the fresh brewer's yeast, the suggested final proof if your ambient temperature is running at about 15°C to 18°C would be 30 minutes, before giving a generous deep slash to allow for the aggressive oven spring expected. Then set into a well-steamed oven with the temperature set at 230°C. Once set, trim the oven temperature to about 215°C until fully baked to your liking, using your now well-trained eye.

If the Mother yeast has been used, then the final proof will be no more than 1 hour, and the procedure for the bake will be very similar to the above.

As explained at the start, this is one of the more difficult flours to perfect, so it's worth making notes as you progress, just to help iron out some of the finer points needed as nature intervenes each year.

PIZZA DOUGH

This opens another can of worms. I have had many opportunities over the years to work at perfecting this product, often within the confines of mass production, and more interestingly with small artisan producers wanting to emulate something as close as possible to the breads they had eaten when visiting mainly southern Italy. I have been encouraged through the latter years to help home producers, as the passion for a lot of men has shifted from barbeque to garden wood-fired oven. So, fortunately, I have many variations, and what follows is a blend of my experiences.

While adding as much fermentation as historically would have used to produce these breads, the favourite method, not surprisingly, is very closely related to the open crumb recipe in the advanced recipe section when producing Ciabatta and Focaccia. The only difference is that no additional water is added on the second stage of the dough. I will give the full recipe again, to avoid confusion, as the treatment of the dough through the final stages is different, but I point this out to help you appreciate how breads have evolved over the years, as bakers travelled around with their skills from country to country, throughout what is now known as Europe.

The beauty of this dough is that you can use it as soon as you have completed the process, or if you wish, you can also store pieces in the fridge for up to three days, ready for a quick lunch whenever you need them. To do so, place a tea towel neatly inside a plastic container with a lid, or cover a baking sheet with it before heavily dusting with semolina. This will ensure they do not stick if left in the fridge for a long period of time. Scale the dough into your preferred weight, scuff up the dough balls to form a nice tight mould and place them onto the baking sheet or into the plastic container, seal or cover and place into the fridge. When needed, just bring out of the fridge 30 minutes before you want to bake; after the recovery time, roughly press out to the preferred circumference, and by the time this has been topped, it will be ready to set into the oven.

PIZZA DOUGH

INGREDIENTS	%	GRAMS
Strong bread flour	100	440
Light rye flour	10	44
Water	80	352
Salt	2	9
Olive oil	1	4.5
Yeast	3	13.5
	Total	863

METHOD

Set down an overnight batter, using these proportions of the ingredients from the list above:

Flour	300
Rye flour	44
Cold water	352
Yeast	6

Beat to a creamy batter and set to one side overnight, ensuring it is covered to avoid skinning.

NEXT DAY ADD

Flour	140
Salt	9
Yeast	7.5

And bring to a full dough, when it is starting to become nice and elastic, add

Olive oil	4.5

Continue to develop until it is clear and silky to the touch.

Total	863

Produces 6 x 125g, 15cm to 20cm (6 to 8 inches) pizzas, depending on how thick you like them.

When the dough is fully developed, you can bulk for just 1 hour before scaling to your required weight, scuff up to form a tight ball and place on a tea towel heavily dusted with semolina or something similar in texture, to rest for 30 minutes before processing. Or refrigerate as above.

I have used the rye Mother as the yeast source in the first stages of the dough with good results, but if you chose to do so you would need to omit the rye flour from the recipe and reduce the water content by 30g to compensate for this change. The fresh yeast on the second stage would still need to be added if using straight away but it is not necessary if you are retarding the dough balls over two or three days in the fridge.

Forgotten Favourites

DOUGH CAKE

No recipe book would be complete without a few sweet treats in it. The Dough cake followed very close behind the Lardy cake. It evolved to avoid waste, as well as to be a little luxury in our leaner times.

Through the week the baker would try to make the right amount of dough for the numbers of loaves ordered, but often because of changes in orders, there would be an excess of dough. This dough would be retained each day and kept in a tub; at the end of the week the dough cake would be made using over-ripe dough.

If you can plan ahead when you make your bread, make an extra amount of dough and keep it at an ambient temperature for 3 or 4 days. If you are starting from scratch, just make up the required amount of dough 3 or 4 days before you want to make the cake.

DOUGH CAKE		
INGREDIENTS	%	GRAMS
Old dough	100	300
Dark sugar	15	45
Mixed spice	1	3
Lard	20	60
Fresh yeast	5	15
Currants	20	60
Mixed peel	5	15
	Total	498

METHOD

Place the lard, sugar and spice into the mixing bowl with a beater attachment, beat to a creamy consistency. Set the beater to run on slow speed and add the dough a small piece at a time; carry on mixing until the dough has roughly dispersed but with rough pieces of dough still visible. Add the yeast and mix for a little longer, then add the currants and mixed peel; continue mixing until evenly dispersed.

This amount of mix will fill a small bread tin, but it is advisable to line the tin with baking parchment first, as it has a tendency to stick, even to a non-stick pan.

Place the mixture into the bread tin and lightly press out to fill the corners. This will require 1 hour to rest, but don't expect it to increase in size too much over this period.

Set the oven to 200°C prior to baking. When the dough cake has had its time, and just before setting into the oven, sprinkle the top heavily with demerara sugar then bake for 35 minutes.

This cake is better eaten fresh or within three days of production; after this it helps to have thick butter on it or try it as a pudding with custard.

VEGETABLE BOBBINS

This product is very close to my heart, as prepping the vegetables for them was one of the jobs I was given when I first started working in the bakery in the evenings after school. In those days basic root vegetables such as swede, parsnip, turnip, carrot and potato were traditionally used, so in the evenings I was sat down on a pile of hessian flour bags (I will give you a little history about our flour bags later) with a rusty old well-worn grater that could take chunks out of the finger tips and knuckles if you lost concentration through repetition and boredom as you worked your way through the bags of vegetables of the day.

The baker spread these over a sheet of dough with a few herbs and lots of pepper and salt, before rolling it all up into a tight roll similar to a Swiss roll or Chelsea bun. He would then chop the roll into generous sized pieces, place them onto a baking sheet with the swirl facing up, sprinkle heavily with grated cheese, prove them for 30 minutes and bake.

Over the years of trying to resurrect this basic product, it has proven difficult to find the right vegetable combination for modern tastes; some people find the traditional choice of vegetables off-putting. They were the cheaper root vegetables, and chosen I assume for that reason, but trust me, they did taste great fresh from the oven on a cold winter's day.

They can be made and filled with almost any vegetable of your choice, and the one that has proven to be more acceptable over the past decade has been cream cheese or tomato puree spread on first, then sprinkled with grated courgette, carrot, yellow pepper and broken walnut, heavily seasoned with a generous sprinkling of herbs added before rolling up. Bean sprouts, celery and rocket went down well with the children.

The dough traditionally used was produced using 100% wholemeal flour, but rather than using 100% wholemeal, try a blend of white and wholemeal, but remember to reduce your liquid to compensate.

TRADITIONAL VEGETABLE BOBBINS		
INGREDIENTS	%	GRAMS
Coarse wholemeal flour	100	500
Salt	2	10
Lard	15	75
Baking powder	3	15
Milk	70	350
Herbs	1	5
Yeast	1	5
	Total	960

METHOD

NOTE

The milk will need to be warmed a little if being used straight from the fridge, and there are benefits to flavour and texture if soured milk is used; I have used buttermilk on occasion.

Blend the yeast with a little of the milk.

Place the flour, salt, herbs and lard into a mixing bowl, and rub the lard roughly through the flour. It will not need to be blended as much as you would for a scone, for example, as we need some of the glutens exposed to create some elasticity in this dough. Add the yeast blend and the remainder of the milk and work to a full dough.

When the dough has reached a silky texture, cover and place in the fridge for 1 hour. While the dough is resting, you can prepare the grated vegetables. I have found that there is a benefit to preparing these just before you build the bobbin, otherwise valuable moistures and vitamins will released and lost from the vegetables if prepared too far in advance, as traditionally done in the bakery. You will need at least 400g of mixed root vegetables grated (reduce that weight to 250g-300g if using courgettes) and in the old days, it would have been just parsnip, swede, turnip, potato and carrot. Once grated, season well with salt and pepper.

Bring the dough from the fridge and place onto a well-floured work surface, pin out to a rectangle of about 30cm by 40cm (12 by 16 inches), ensuring the dough is free-flowing and not stuck to the work surface. Wash a strip along the bottom edge with a little water to ensure it sticks once rolled up, then spread the remaining surface evenly with the prepared vegetables, pressing them lightly into the dough.

Starting from the top, roll down in Swiss roll style, stretching the dough upwards each time you roll down. This action will ensure it is rolled as tight as you can, so that the vegetables don't fall out when cut into individual pieces.

Once completed, and before cutting, mark out to make sure you have 12 equal sized pieces. When you are happy they are all the same size, cut through, and place onto a baking sheet with the swirl side facing up, making sure they are well spaced, giving them room to spread as they bake.

These will need to sit, covered, for about 30 minutes to recover; while waiting, you will have time to grate a little strong Cheddar cheese. This needs to be placed generously onto each bobbin, covering the exposed vegetables on the top side, just before setting into a preheated oven set at 220°C.

The bake on these products needs to be light, to ensure the vegetables still have a crunch, and about 20 to 25 minutes is a good guide.

Back to the flour bags

Historically in the UK, all flour was delivered in hessian flour bags, and luckily for me, before my time the standard weight for a bag of flour was 280 lbs, or in modern weight 128 kilos. This was one very large bag of flour, and it would be delivered to the bakery on a trailer, and hoisted into the bakery loft using a pulley suspended from a beam over the loft door. The baker would then wobble this onto a pair of sack wheels, and wheel it across to place it in the right position for storage in the loft. When it was needed, the baker would then wobble it across to the flour chute situated over the dough mixer, cut the string on the top of the sack, and shoot it down through a fabric chute into the bowl. The result of this drop engulfed the whole of the bakery and the bakers below in a cloud of fine flour dust.

This weight of 280 lbs of flour became the recognised weight for a volume of bread, so it logically became known as a sack of bread in the industry. A sack of bread would produce 220 2lb loaves or 140 4lb loaves, known as quarterns. These were for hotels and the catering trade. Machinery and equipment such as ovens, dough troughs when doughs were mixed by hand, and later the limited range of mechanical mixers, were manufactured to produce this volume of bread. For instance, the faggot oven I cut my teeth on was known as a sack oven because a good baker could set 220 loaves into this one chamber in one bake.

The old Dumbril single-arm mixer, which would groan and clonk with every stroke of the arm for at least 25 minutes every morning to complete one mix, was known as a two-sack mixer, as it was capable of mixing two of those 280 lbs bags of flour into a dough on one mix. A mix this size would make it possible for a baker to produce two full ovens in one go; the first bake would be for the softer baked products such as the batch breads, sister bricks and light bakes. The second bake, as it had fermented for two hours longer, would produce the crusty breads such as the Bloomers, Coburgs and Cottage. Even these would be taken off and handed up for their intermediate proof times, and this extra time created the different tastes required on each named loaf. The bowl on this mixer was massive, making it impossible to reach into it to cut the dough out. Starting was all right, as the dough had proven up and some days even started to erupt over the edge, making it easy to cut off large chunks to throw over to the baker on the scaling table. The difficulty came when you were half way down the bowl. By now you were standing on tiptoe to reach in. You had to judge it just right, as you now needed to pull a pin underneath to be able to tilt the bowl forward. If it tilted too soon, it became a panic, trying to cut the dough off in larger and larger chunks to keep up with it as it rushed to get out of the bowl.

By the time I started in the bakery, it had sensibly been decided to reduce the size of these sacks, I assume for the wellbeing of the baker, and also the poor delivery man, even before Health and Safety became involved. So the sack size was halved, making 140 lbs, or 64 kilos in today's world. This became known as a bag of flour. Now two bags equalled one sack. This wasn't such a smart move, as now the flour was stored downstairs and not in the loft, so to prove yourself to be a macho baker, you had to be able to pick one of these bags up by hugging it like a bear, waddle over to the mixer, giving one hefty heave up to rest it onto the side of the bowl, cut the tie without losing the string into the flour as the first half of the bag cascaded quickly into the bowl, while ensuring the bottom half of the bag that was resting on your raised knee didn't fall back to the floor, as there was certainly a point of no return as you learnt this art, much to the amusement of the older lads in the bakery.

The hessian bags were very valuable, so a deposit of four shillings was charged on them to ensure that they were returned with each new delivery. It would be true to say my boss was a very careful man where money was concerned, and there were many things I would be asked to do for him to save money that would make you cringe in today's sterile world. My last job on a Saturday was one of them. I would have to take the complete week's stock of empty flour bags, which had been discarded on the floor in the corner of the bakery, stand on a box so I could reach over the bowl of the Dumbril mixer, turn each bag inside out and then starting from the top of the bag work my way down, shaking out all the flour that was still clinging to the hessian bag, fold them neatly, placing nine into one bag, ready for a credit note to be raised on their return. The amount of flour captured this way was very small and I often wondered if it was worth the risk, as I picked out many foreign bodies that had made their home in these bags over the week. Obviously by the time I had finished, I was completely covered from head to toe in flour. Despite the cloud of dust that I left behind me as I cycled my way home, Mum was never overjoyed with the problems the residue of flour in my clothes caused her on Monday's washing day, as a washing machine was unheard of luxury for a farm worker's family. As a consequence, and despite Mum's efforts, all my working clothes accumulated these hard bobbles attached to them.

For some of the speciality breads produced, imported flours such as the Canadian flours would be added sparingly by the baker, as they were very costly. These were originally milled in their home country and then shipped across in their own bags, made of a very fine woven linen-type material, rather than the wheat in containers as it is today. These bags were much better to handle and had many uses, hence a black market soon sprang up, so by the end of the week there were very few of these bags left to shake. No one seemed to know where they disappeared to, much to the dismay of the boss and his loss of the deposit.

Through the late sixties and early seventies, hessian bags were slowly phased out, being replaced with paper to prevent contamination. The bag size was also once again reduced, taking them down to 70 lbs or 32 kilos, as the awareness of Health and Safety became necessary. (Strangely enough, bakers will be bakers, so the challenge then became to see if you could now carry two of these on your shoulder when moving them around.) This was still known as a quarter sack in the baking world, making four of these to one sack, so all the other calculations within the baking industry worked well with this change.

The next big change came when European law started trying to interfere, enforcing European weight controls for Health and Safety reasons upon our industry, so now nobody could carry more than 25 kilos, and the Continental recognised weight was traditionally 100 kilo units. By this time I was on the road, selling flour, so I was at the coal face, so to speak. This change caused major problems to the smaller, and indeed some of the larger, bakers who had managed to survive, creating a little rebellion as all the calculations passed down over the years would need to be changed. It is strange that many of our baking skills have disappeared over the years with little or no challenge in our quest for speed and mass production, but our weights and volumes have remained and became a standing point, as so many recipes and calculations would have needed to be changed. As a result of this solidarity, there was a brief time of confusion, as the millers tried to conform, but the baking industry seems to have won this little victory, as a lot of the flour is now delivered to the craft baker in 16 kilo bags, making eight of these to the historic sack weight used by my Granddad. Let's hope this camaraderie within our trade continues, with our new-found baking skills being passed on throughout the new generation of up-and-coming passionate bakers. This will ensure our trade never sinks to the levels experienced through the dark years.

It is obvious that my chosen industry has to be continually changing to evolve for the better, as it has over the relatively short time of fifty-plus years I have been privileged to work with it. Over these so few years, it has occurred to me that I am still on a learning curve. As I answer one question, another will make itself apparent to me. I have learnt the hard way never to assume I have conquered this craft, as if I do, I quickly stagnate and the quality I seek in the finished article soon deteriorates. I feel that if I was privileged enough to be given another fifty years to continue to develop my knowledge, it still wouldn't be enough time to profess to being an expert. So much of my time in the early years was spent re-inventing the wheel, continually looking for information my forefathers already knew and held in their hands, but little of it was ever written down, as it was just bread. I can only sow the seeds, in hope of encouraging the next generation, to make them grow and continually improve their knowledge to pass on to others.

Appendix: Ash Content

Ash content is a figure used to ascertain the quality and colour of a flour throughout Europe. For example, in a rye flour a typical range used will be, say, a 700 ash for a very light colour. This is achieved by extracting a lot of the bran, using probably only 55% to 60% of the berry. This flour will take less water as the bran content is lower.

Normally this flour is used for the whiter breads and confectionery. Most of the European rye breads are produced using a medium ash, around 997, with a higher bran content, normally very finely ground to obtain colour rather than texture, as with our brown flours. A wholemeal version of rye flour will carry a figure of around 1350, and the particle size is normally slightly larger. These flours demand a much higher water content as the bran content is higher.

There are many other variations of this throughout a flour range, as individual bakers and millers set their specifications.

The figure is ascertained by burning off a set amount of the flour being tested in a furnace set at 2000°C for a set time. The ash left will define the protein and colour of each flour sample.

France and Italy work to the same rules, hence the T55, T85 and so on for France, and the commonly requested Italian oo that anything made to an Italian recipe seems, in my opinion too foolishly, to recommend. oo was originally formulated for fresh pasta only. If you use a standard white flour for this product, it will have very fine specks of bran still in it. Although not visible to the eye when the dough is freshly mixed, as it ages the specks will become visible as the pH in the dough changes with age. This creates a greyish background with prominent brown specks. This also takes place in puff pastry if it is kept at an ambient temperature and the correct flour isn't used. Making a flour to this specification is extremely expensive and wasteful, as 55% of the grain will go to animal feed. There is little point in using a pristine white oo flour to produce a product that you add other ingredients to, such as pizza or Ciabatta or similar breads.

"A big thank you for a lovely day's bread making today. I found it most interesting and informative, and your excellent presentation made it an enjoyable experience. I hadn't realised there was so much to know about bread making and the various flours and raising agents. I will never take bread for granted again....

"I have been on quite a few different courses and can honestly say that your course was one of the best I have been on. Your passion for what you do is infectious and has inspired me to have a go at 'proper' breadmaking without the aid of my bread maker – and using fresh yeast."

Susan

Index

Your Notes

Lightning Source UK Ltd.
Milton Keynes UK
UKOW07f0841010216

267509UK00002B/5/P